CU01021914

A Pictorial C

THE MOUNTAINS C

1. The Northern Peaks

A Pictorial Guide to

THE MOUNTAINS OF SNOWDONIA

1. The Northern Peaks

JOHN GILLHAM

FRANCES LINCOLN LIMITED

PUBLISHERS

To my dear wife Nicola
who accompanied me on so many of the trips

The author intends to keep this book as up-to-date as possible,
and will offer information updates on his website:
www.johngillham.com

Frances Lincoln Limited
4 Torriano Mews
Torriano Avenue
London NW5 2RZ

A Pictorial Guide to the Mountains of Snowdonia
Volume 1. The Northern Peaks
Copyright © 2010 Frances Lincoln Limited

Text, photographs and 3D sketch maps
copyright © 2010 John Gillham
Edited by Roly Smith
Designed by Jane Havell Associates
First Frances Lincoln edition 2010

John Gillham has asserted his moral right to be
identified as Author of this Work in accordance
with the Copyright, Designs and Patents Act 1988

Mapping data licensed from Ordnance Survey®
with permission of HMSO.
© Crown copyright 2009. All rights reserved.
Ordnance Survey Licence number 100043293

British Library cataloguing-in-publication data
A catalogue record for this book is available from
the British Library
ISBN 978-0-7112-2973-0
Printed and bound in China
9 8 7 6 5 4 3 2 1

Frontispiece: Approach to Llyn Edno beneath
Moel Meirch in the Nantgwynant Hills
Title page map: Tryfan

Contents

CONTENTS

CONTENTS

The Northern Peaks

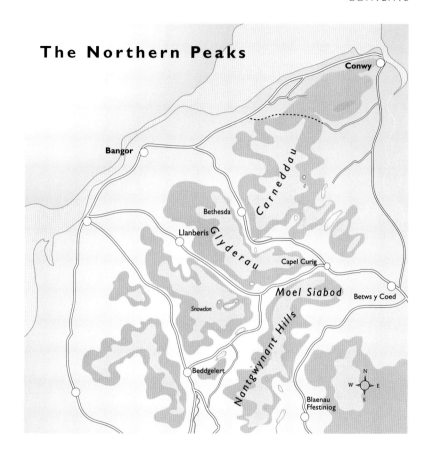

Conwy

Bangor

Carneddau

Bethesda

Llanberis

Glyderau

Capel Curig

Moel Siabod

Betws y Coed

Snowdon

Nantgwynant Hills

Beddgelert

N
W E
S

Blaenau
Ffestiniog

> *To myself, mountains are the beginning and end of all*
> *natural scenery: in them, and in forms of inferior landscape*
> *that lead to them, my affections are wholly bound up.*
> JOHN RUSKIN, MODERN PAINTERS (1888)

I've had a very mundane week that's never been far away from the darned computer and the world of Ruskin's inferior landscapes, so I'm escaping up the A5 towards the real world and the Welsh mountains. Snowdonia's been on my mind since Tuesday. The coach-loads of tourists in the trinket shops of Betws-y-coed, a sort of Blackpool in the trees, are behind me now and the road weaves through woodland and pasture. A few houses, a garage and some interesting-looking pubs line the roadside, then there's a gaggle of shops at a road junction.

This is Capel Curig, a straggling village with all the amenities for a good weekend's walking. Morning life in Capel centres on the Pinnacle Café, especially if there's rain about. I stop for a break. Today there's a gathering of walkers and climbers studying the world over the crust of a bacon butty and the steam from a mug of tea. Through the raindrops on the windowpane I can see there's now grey clag where Moel Siabod should be. But I've got to get up into the mountains!

At Nant Peris there's a smell of pines on the breeze, combining with wet grass. The lower crags of Esgair Felen are black and dripping; the upper ones are in the gods and out of sight. The steep path I'm on is heading for those low clouds, while the Afon Las on my left is scurrying down in white-water torrents, desperate to get down to the sanctuary of Nant Peris. I soon realise that it's escaping from the sleet, which had been hiding in those clouds and is now falling ever-so-delicately on to my nose and melting into trickles down my neck.

The hills disappear into the white mist and I decide that the easier ground of Y Garn is a better bet than my original idea of Glyder Fawr. I make the summit at p.m. and take comfort in my flask of tea. The snow god has switched off the view

Opposite: Ledge path near Aber Falls.

15

into Nant Ffrancon – all I see are the lightly frosted blades of grass beneath my feet; but I'm just happy to be here.

Back down the hill I meet somebody coming out of the Vaynol Arms. He sees the raindrops on the end of my nose and my shiny bedraggled waterproofs and says, 'Rather you than me, mate!'

Inspired in the early days by the books of Poucher and Wainwright, I have walked to most of the English and Welsh summits and in many of the Alpine regions of Europe. But Snowdonia has always been my favourite, probably because I'm half-Welsh on my mother's side, but mainly because of its mountains: when I want to walk, I can choose from scores of majestic peaks – from the Conwy to the Dyfi rivers; from the heights of Snowdon to little 'half-day' rock knolls like Carreg-y-saeth in the Rhinogs.

Although Snowdonia is not as prettily dressed up with pastures, woods or cottage gardens as the Lake District and it's not as wild as Scotland, it shares many of the best attributes of both places – and in just the right measure. Also, Snowdonia is not too big to be inaccessible nor too small for peak-baggers' tick lists. Having National Park status, it is not subjected to too many unsympathetic developments, although the park boundaries cleverly sneak away from those awful slate quarries.

This is the first book of four and covers Northern Snowdonia – the Carneddau, the Glyderau and the Nantgwynant ranges. These three mountain ranges are very different from each other and present their own opportunities and problems.

The Carneddau are the Cairngorms of Wales, albeit on a smaller scale. They are a complex system of grassy and stony ridges and spurs radiating from one central spine and cover an expansive area, from the beaches of Conwy Bay to the Ogwen and Llugwy valleys, and from the Menai Straits to the Conwy Valley. In the south the Carneddau are higher and more bouldery, with their northern faces scoured by glaciers into cliffs, crags and gullies. In the north they're wilder, grassier, and with more remote feel.

The Glyderau peaks face the Carneddau across Nant Ffrancon and the Llugwy valley. They're compact, rugged and more random in their sculptural makeup. All the great mountain features are there: corries, arêtes, tarns, ridges and waterfalls, but I have to admit they're more Giacometti than Henry Moore.

Less well known are the mountains of Nantgwynant, the ones between Moel Sia-bod above Capel Curig and Cnicht above Beddgelert. Moel Siabod itself is a mighty peak with two fine ridges and a rocky arête providing a sporty ascent to the summit that is akin to Striding Edge on Helvellyn. The ridges to its south are knobbly; grassy in some places, heathery in others. Jewel-like tarns are scattered all over the ridge – this is excellent backpacking country – and the ever-changing views of Snowdon and its Horseshoe walk are a joy to behold as you work your way over rocky bluffs.

Cnicht, the knight, is the southern sentry keeping watch over the deep, quarried chasms of Cwmorthin and Cwm Croesor. Seen from the west Cnicht appears as an almost perfect Matterhorn, and the final stages of the climb from this direction are sporting and memorable. The Nantgwynant mountains may not have any 3000-foot-ers among their ranks, but scenically they are up there with the best.

Below: Yr Elen in the wilds of the Carneddau seen from Cwm Caseg.

Volume Two of this series will include Snowdon, the highest and most famous mountain in Wales, along with two not so well-known ranges, the Rhinogydd and Eifionydd. The former have been hewn from Cambrian grits older than any of the other Welsh mountains, while the latter have been fashioned by volcanoes and lava flows. Both offer enchanting seldom-trod routes for the connoisseur of fine scenery.

Volume Three will cover Eastern Snowdonia. The Migneint is wilderness, more than any other area of the National Park – it's for lovers of solitude and wet feet. Only slightly less remote are the larger and rockier Arenig Mountains. The Moelwynion and Ffestiniog peaks have been ravaged but not tamed by the quarrymen and the miners. The sense of history is heightened as you pass long-abandoned barracks and the remains of old tramway bogies and pulleys. Finally, there are the long ridges and glacial rocky cwms of the Berwyns. Most of the peaks of the range are outside the National Park but they're too near, too big and too beautiful to be ignored.

Volume Four includes Cadair Idris, the Dyfi Hills, the Aran range and the Tarren Hills – here you will be able to walk some of the longest ridges in Wales.

In the books I will try to cover all the hills and mountains that are of interest to the walker. Some will be famous; others will not.

Let's hope that Snowdonia and its mountains bring to you, the reader, as much joy as they have done to me.

I've divided the book up into three sections, one for each mountain range. For each mountain I've given various routes to the top, followed by ridge routes to the next peak. This allows readers to devise their own combinations of routes. The routes are numbered within each section, and the corresponding numbers are marked in yellow circles on the location maps at the beginning of each section. At the end of the section for each mountain range I've added a couple of big day-walks – usually, but not always, circular routes. These will take in the best of the mountains and also add some low-level link routes. If there's anything special to watch out for, I've added notes on route-finding in descent.

The panoramic drawings are not to scale and are no substitute for the recommended use of OS Explorer or Harvey maps. In the interests of clarity, I've often raised or lowered a ridge and pulled 'out of sight' detail to the right or left a tad. Artistic licence is my advantage over modern digital imaging: I can see around a bend.

All the routes are safe for experienced walkers in clement conditions, but in wintry conditions even some of the most innocuous routes become dangerous and may be impassable. If these conditions are possible, take an ice axe and crampons, but first make sure you know how to use them. Be ready to turn around where necessary. A few routes, such as the Snowdon Horseshoe, Tryfan's North Ridge and the Bristly Ridge, are Grade 1 scrambles and shouldn't be attempted by the inexperienced or by those without a good head for heights or sense of balance. Anything above Grade 1 I've left for more specialist books.

Remember, too, even the mountains change. A storm could have brought down a path across loose mountain scree or friable terrain; a bridge could have been washed away by those storms, or operations of some sort or another could have necessitated a diversion or closure of a path. River crossings can become difficult or even impossible after periods of snow or heavy rainfall and conifer plantations are forever changing. Trees reach maturity and whole blocks are felled leaving behind hard-to-follow or diverted footpaths. Always be prepared to adjust your itinerary.

Overleaf: One of the grand mountainscapes of Snowdonia seen from Y Garn. Here, Llyn Ogwen, Llyn Idwal and Llyn Clyd, three lakes on different levels, are flanked by the peaks of Tryfan and Glyder Fach.

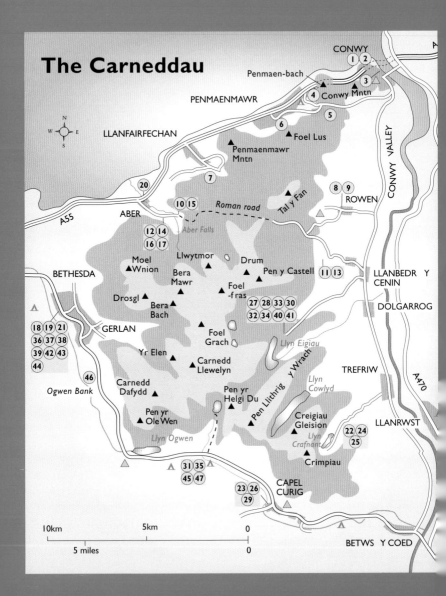

The Carneddau

CONWY
①②
③
Penmaen-bach
PENMAENMAWR
④ Conwy Mntn
⑤
⑥ ▲ Foel Lus
LLANFAIRFECHAN
▲ Penmaenmawr Mntn
⑦
⑧⑨
ROWEN
⑳
▲ Tal y Fan
⑩⑮ *Roman road*
ABER
A55
Aber Falls
⑫⑭
⑯⑰
Moel ▲Wnion
Llwytmor
▲ Drum
Pen y Castell
⑪⑬
LLANBEDR Y CENIN
BETHESDA
Bera Mawr ▲
▲ Foel -fras
DOLGARROG
Drosgl ▲
Bera Bach ▲
②⑦②⑧③③③⓪
③②③④④⓪④①
Llyn Eigiau
⑱⑲㉑
㊱㊲㊳
㊴㊷㊸
㊹
GERLAN
Foel Grach
Yr Elen ▲
▲ Carnedd Llewelyn
Llyn Cowlyd
TREFRIW
A470
⑯
Ogwen Bank
Carnedd Dafydd ▲
Pen yr Helgi Du ▲
Creigiau Gleision
LLANRWST
Pen yr ▲ Ole Wen
Llyn Ogwen
Pen Llithrig y Wrach
Llyn Crafnant
㉒㉔
㉕
③①③⑤
㊺㊼
▲ Crimpiau
㉓㉖
㉙
CAPEL CURIG
BETWS Y COED

10km   5km   0
5 miles   0

The Carneddau are the most expansive range in Wales, covering an area of around 85 square miles/ 22,000 ha, more than Snowdon and the Glyderau put together. The main ridge rises from the sands at Conwy and stretches 14 miles/ 23km to the shores of Llyn Ogwen. Subsidiary ridges radiate to the coast, the Conwy Valley, and the Ogwen and Llugwy valleys to form long cwms, few of which are cultivated or inhabited to any great degree.

Although they're parcelled by the A5, the A55 and A470 highways, no major roads make incursions to the Carnedd mountains. Only the narrowest country lanes climb to the foothills – they're ideal for walkers who want to gain a bit of height and distance before donning their boots. Seven of the fifteen Welsh 3000-foot peaks are here: in fact between Pen yr Ole Wen in the south and Foel-fras in the north, the Carneddau spine rarely drops below the 3000-foot mark.

The Peaks

Main Tops	height	
Carnedd Llewelyn	3489ft	1064m
Carnedd Dafydd	3426ft	1044m
Pen yr Ole Wen	3207ft	978m
Foel Grach	3201ft	976m
Yr Elen	3155ft	962m
Foel-fras	3089ft	942m
Llwytmor	2784ft	849m
Pen yr Helgi Du	2732ft	833m
Bera Bach	2646ft	807m
Bera Mawr	2604ft	794m
Pen Llithrig y Wrach	2591ft	790m
Drum	2525ft	770m
Drosgl	2486ft	758m
Creigiau Gleision	2223ft	678m
Pen y Castell	2043ft	623m
Tal y Fan	2000ft	610m
Moel Wnion	1902ft	580m
Crimpiau	1558ft	475m
Alltwen (Conwy Mountain)	836ft	255m
Penmaen-bach (Conwy Mountain)	804ft	245m
Mynydd y Dref (Conwy Mountain)	800ft	244m

Carneddau means cairns, referring to Iron and Bronze Age burial sites. One look at the map reveals the extent of these ancient civilizations, for on many of the hilltops, especially those of the north, are the words 'fort', 'burial mound', 'hut circle', 'stone circle'. The last of these civilizations, the Ordovices, would have farmed on the upper Carneddau slopes when the Romans came.

Although these proud Celtic tribesmen resisted with all the resources they could muster, they were defeated by Julius Agricola somewhere between AD75 and 77. The Ordovices would have had to watch from the hilltops as the invaders built their powerful fort, Canovium, at Caerhun in the Conwy Valley and the road across the mountain pass of Bwlch y Ddeufaen to their fort at Segontium (Caernarfon). After a period of further resistance Agricola ordered his troops to exterminate the Ordovices, and it is believed that he succeeded, for history has no further mention of them.

Although Carneddau ridges let you stay higher for longer and lead you to remote places that give you a little of the wilderness experience, they have never been as popular as neighbouring ranges. Perhaps that's because the Carneddau choose to keep their spectacular bits to themselves. Drive down the A5 and all you'll see of them are grassy whalebacks; drive down the A55 and you'll see pastoral foothills, while from the A470 you'll see pasture and forest.

So let's get our boots on and see for ourselves. In the north we can follow the crowds down to the Aber Falls. It's a spectacular scene, but where's that remoteness? The answer is beyond those screes to the left. We leave the crowds and within half an hour we've entered this empty but beautiful hanging valley. There are wild horses on the ridge, and a mountain, Bera Mawr, with a rugged crest and rocks to clamber over.

Deeper, further, higher we go . . . a new valley appears, long and sickle-shaped and with two great peaks on the far side. This higher of the two is the monarch of the Carneddau, Carnedd Llewelyn. Craggy and dome-shaped, this Colossus is named after Llewelyn the Great, 13th-century Prince of Wales. Like Snowdon's highest summit, Yr Wyddfa, it is the hub of the range, throwing out four distinct ridges. The shortest but most delectable is the narrow rocky arête to Yr Elen, a more slender and angular peak with crags and screes flowing down to one of Snowdonia's tiniest tarns, Ffynnon Caseg.

Opposite: Part of the stone circle on Cefn Llechen in the northern Carneddau.

Behind Carnedd Llewelyn is Carnedd Dafydd. Now we see the climbers' crags for the first time. Ringed around the head of Cwm Llafar are the great cliffs of Ysgolion Du, which means the black ladders, and Lech-du, with the rocky crest of Crib Lem rising from a tight, bouldery cwm.

The northern faces of the main Carneddau peaks, all unseen from any road, have been sculpted by the ice ages to buttresses, gulleys and cwms. By taking the little lane into Cwm Eigiau, we can seek them out. Past a sullen reservoir with a sad tale to tell, past some high broken precipices, we enter the inner heartlands that once reverberated to the sound of quarrymen, their picks and their gunpowder.

Around the corner, beneath two craggy pyramids, one known as the witch's slide, the other the hill of the black hound, we ease to the head of the cwm. Here is the most spectacular sight in all the Carneddau, Craig yr Ysfa, where a daunting chasm known as the Amphitheatre and its long scree gully lie between giant buttresses. More often than not, the scene will be afforded its grand scale by the diminutive, far-off figures of climbers inching towards the top.

Walkers can always find a way around the Carneddau crags, and here is no different. The slopes of heather and crag to the left of Craig yr Ysfa look impossibly steep, but we'll follow the climbers towards the crags and, sure enough, a tiny path breaks off left, zigzagging up to a high pass – but don't look down!

Finding these mountain passes is part of the joy of the mountains, and the complex of ridges, saddles and cwms make the Carneddau especially pleasurable. Those broad, free-striding ridges have their dangers, though: in hill fog all scale is lost and one ridge looks just like another. It's all too easy to end up in the wrong valley if you don't take your compass. Built in to the summit crags of Foel Grach is a refuge hut which has a log book filled with stories of lost souls.

But I don't want to end on a negative. There's so much good stuff I haven't mentioned yet – the little-known panorama path that rounds the rim of the glen above the Aber Falls, the stunning heather-and-crag scenery of little Crimpiau, the bracing salt air experience of Penmaen-bach . . .

Opposite: Looking down the Amphitheatre Buttress above Cwm Eigiau. These crags are a favoured place for climbers.

MYNYDD Y DREF (CONWY MOUNTAIN)

'Mountain' is a big word for this little hill, but rising with attitude from the waves of the Irish Sea, Mynydd y Dref's steep, crag-fringed slopes defy you to ignore them: the mountains of Snowdonia begin and end here.

Rising from the town walls of Conwy, Mynydd y Dref is part of a four-mile coastal ridge which eventually eases down to the Sychnant Pass, a twisting shaly gorge that separates the hill from the higher Carneddau peaks. Unlike some of its neighbours, the mountain hasn't been totally disfigured by quarrying, though there are the grassed-over remains of past excavations on the northern slopes, just above Conwy's caravan site. The undulating ridge offers splendid easy-striding promenades on grassy ribbons and firm stony paths that cut a dash through heather, stunted gorse and bilberry.

Mynydd y Dref reaches its highest point, 800ft/244m, at Castell Caer Seion, an ancient fort that has been linked with both Roman and Iron Age settlers. Covering an area of around 10 acres/4ha, the fort's formidable man-made ramparts overlook spectacular sea cliffs on one side, and a wide view of the Conwy Valley and the Carneddau mountains to the south. While the Celtic warriors might have been watching for Roman soldiers, you can take advantage of the more peaceful views of Conwy Castle, the town walls, Llandudno's limestone promontory, the Great Orme and Anglesey, which lies across the extensive sands of Lavan.

Penmaen-bach lies to the west of Mynydd y Dref, separated from it by a narrow sliver of farmland. Seen from Dwygyfylchi, it has tremendous crags and screes, not to mention a 600m tunnel allowing the A55 expressway to pass through. The summit is a confusing complex of rocky and heather knolls, many vying for the top spot. Wherever you choose for your views, you'll be impressed by the sweeping seascape towards Llandudno and the Great Orme.

The Conwy Estuary (opposite) and Conwy Castle (right) from the slopes of Mynydd y Dref.

29

Route C1
Direct Route from the Old Coast Road

A very steep but satisfying route

Start: Old Coast Road, Conwy
  (GR: SH 762783)
Distance: 1 mile/1.6km
Height gain: 790ft/240m
Time: ¾ hour

Go over the ladder stile near the road end and veer left around the small quarried rockface. A faint, sandy track now heads straight up the slope, keeping slightly left of a huge crag on the horizon. Although the route is very steep it's quite safe in ascent unless snow or ice prevail. Ignore all of the cross-paths until you come to a wide track just below the previously mentioned crag. Here you can either continue on the faint path to the ridge (Route C1a) or take a breather and turn left along the track. The track soon degenerates into a narrow path which eases to the ridge where a turn right along the well-defined ridge path will join Route C1a on a delightful promenade to the summit fort.

Route C2
Quarry Route from the Old Coast Road

A less steep alternative, using an old tramway

Start: Old Coast Road, Conwy
  (GR: SH 762783)
Distance: 1¼ miles/1.9km
Height gain: 790ft/240m
Time: 1 hour

As in Route C1, go over the ladder stile but this time turn right across the field at the foot of the mountain before climbing towards the tramways on a path weaving through gorse bushes. Grass tramways linking the old pulley houses lead steadily up the mountainside. On reaching the top pulley house, continue along a path heading for the dam of a small quarry reservoir. Although it's almost non-existent to start with, a faint path can soon be seen leading the route from the tree-ringed reservoir through a wide, bracken-filled hollow to a dip in the skyline ridge. Here you turn left on a stony path to the summit fort.

Right: Castell Caer Sion, an ancient hilltop fortress on Mynydd y Dref. Covering an area of 4 hectares, it has been associated with both Roman and Iron Age settlers.

bove: Llandudno and the Conwy estuary seen from Route C1 up the slopes of Mynydd y Dref.

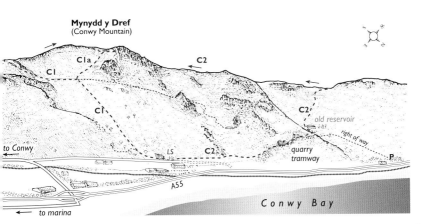

Route C3

Conwy Marina

A pleasing route taking in the castle,
waterfront and mountain

Start: Beacons car park (near yacht marina),
Conwy (GR: SH 772789)

Distance: 2¼ miles/3.5km

Height gain: 820ft/250m

Time: 1½ hours

Follow the road to the marina, turn left to round the waterfront, then right to pass the pub. On the far side of the pub's car park, turn right along the road, then next left to cross the bridge over the dual carriageway and past the school. Cross the old coast road and the railway by a footbridge.

Beyond this, a lane skirts the woods of Coed Ffridd and takes the route round the eastern fringes of Conwy Mountain to meet Mountain Road from Cadnant Park, which joins from the left. Turn right along this road, passing an old quarry entrance and a couple of houses. Beyond the houses a footpath way-marker guides you on to a path on the right, which goes over a stile and rakes up hillsides studded with gorse and twisted hawthorns.

North Wales Coast Path waymarkers high-light a wide grass path traversing the southern flanks of the mountain, but the best route takes a bolder course on to the skyline ridge from where there are stunning views back to the town, its castle and the Conwy estuary. A network of undulating paths criss-cross the ridge but by keeping to the highest you'll come to the summit, crowned by that fasci-nating fort.

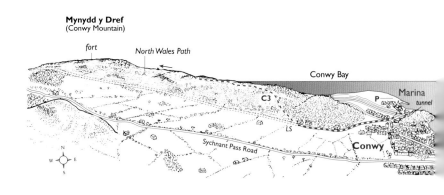

Opposite: Many old quarry tracks criss-cross the sea-facing slopes of Mynydd y Dref.

Above: The Sychnant Pass provides shortcut routes of little ascent to several of the coastal peaks, including Alltwen, seen here on the right.

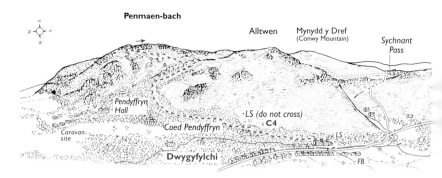

Route C4
Penmaen-bach and Dwygyflchi

*A splendid little route through woodland
    and heather*
Start: Sychnant Pass road, Dwygyfylchi
    (GR: SH 742769)
Distance: 1¼ miles/2km
Height gain: 720ft/220m
Time: 1 hour

Go over the footbridge then turn right down a streamside track. At the end of the track turn left along a footpath behind terraced houses, before going right up some steps. Now a lovely path climbs through mixed woodland. A marker post highlights a zigzag path to the top of the woods. Don't cross the ladder stile but follow the path alongside the fence.

About 100m after going through a gate, take a right fork path climbing steep grass slopes through a pine plantation. At the top continue over heather slopes before turning until you reach a narrow path running across the col between Alltwen and Penmaen-bach. Turn right if you want to bag Alltwen first (return to this same spot if you do); otherwise, turn left towards the craggy slopes of Penmaen-bach. Ignore the paths rounding the fields of Pen-pyra but take the left fork path which rakes up the rock and scree slopes of Penmaen-bach, rounding them to the high north side. The path fades, but you turn right up a heathery hollow to reach the top.

For those who want to continue to the fort on Mynydd y Dref, a path over crag and grass descends to meet a farm track at the west side of two small pastured fields. This continues around the rim of a wide, quarried cwm. There are many tracks but the best follows Route C2 on the stony path climbing directly to Conwy Mountain's summit.

Other route options

I've listed two routes from the coast to Mynydd y Dref but there are many more, using old quarry tracks and informal tourists' direct scrambles. There are also several short options from the Sychnant (dry stream) Pass, a well-known beauty spot where a twisting country lane threads between the pallid brown screes and crags of Alltwen and Maen Esgob on its way down to the green, green grass of Dwygyfylchi's cow pastures. The scene is enlivened in August by blooming heather. A stony track rounds the head of the pass before arcing right across the shoulder of Alltwen to reach the high fields of Pen-pyra. A well-used path begins on the left just before the farm complex and climbs the heather slopes to Alltwen.

For Conwy Mountain: on reaching Pen-pyra's fields maintain direction to cross grass-land – a couple of North Wales Coast Path waymarkers guide you north-east to a small pool where you turn right along another track. You will soon see a small lake over the wall on the right. Just beyond take the broad track diverting left which climbs to the cairn that marks the path to the summit.

PENMAENMAWR MOUNTAIN

I was looking at my 1947 one-inch OS map and was surprised to see Penmaenmawr had a nice rounded summit then, 1550ft above the waves of Conwy Bay. Earlier maps would have shown a great fort, Braich y Dinas, but it was sacked, not by the Romans, but by early 20th-century quarrymen. Today there's nothing left, and the nice little dome has been flattened then exploded to reveal a huge crater. The 'summit' is not the highest place any more.

It's partly your fault, of course: if you brought your car or caught the train to Wales you'll have almost certainly been over a little bit of Penmaenmawr Mountain – the hard granite from the hill was used for road surfacing and as a trackbed for the railway. In better times the peak would have had a fine rock-face, just like Penmaen-bach but higher and grander, and it would have had magnificent views to the high Carneddau. Today, walkers can't get to this summit without being confronted by JCBs and signs warning you about the CCTV cameras.

Below: Penmaenmawr Mountain and Pemaenmawr town seen from the slopes of Foel Lus.

Tal y Fan translates as 'end peak', quite appropriate as it's the most northerly Welsh 2000-footer. Dominant from the Conwy estuary, its ruffled craggy summit rises gracefully from the sandbars of the river in lush green pastures, scattered woods and lonely farms. The mountain is the highest point of a 4 mile/6.5km ridge stretching between Bwlch y Ddeufaen in the south-west and the Sychnant Pass in the north-east.

Tal y Fan is separated from its slightly lower twin peak, Foel Lwyd, by a shallow saddle of moorland. Both summits are rocky, the latter slightly less so, and both are interspersed with carpets of heather and bilberry. Luckily, the hardy Welsh sheep have ensured a good supply of smooth grassland is available for comfortable walking. Although not spectacular, Tal y Fan has much to recommend it.

It's only three miles from the coast but a sense of isolation is heightened by the vast, empty plateau separating the main ridge and the shapely coastal knolls, which block out

Below: Tal y Fan ridge to Foel Lwyd.

most signs of modern civilization. Conwy's Castle just peeps out from behind the moors, while the limestone isthmus of the Great Orme stretches across the waves of the Irish Sea. In the opposite direction lie the even more remote whalebacks of the central Carneddau.

The whole environs of Tal y Fan are scattered with ancient history – standing stones, ancient hut circles and burial chambers. Ordovician tribesmen would have farmed the plateau. Looking south from the summit you'll see lines of pylons and a stony track weaving its way though the mountains. This is an ancient highway used by Roman troops marching to and from forts at Segontium (Caernarfon) and Canovium (Caerhun) in the Conwy Valley.

On a busy summer Sunday or bank holiday, when the world is walking the well-worn paths of Snowdon and the other 3000-foot peaks, why not give the quiet expanses of Tal y Fan a go?

Below: Tal y Fan summit.

Route C5
From the Sychnant Pass

A long but easy stroll through ancient history
Start: Sychnant Pass above Dwygyfylchi
   (GR: SH 750769)
Distance: 3¼ miles/6 km
Height gain: 1540ft/510m
Time: 2½ hours

From the car park at the pass, go through the tall stone gateposts on the west side of the road. Through the gate, a cart rack traces a tall stone wall surrounding a pine wood.

A North Wales Path waymarker highlights the point where you should leave the track for a path, which doubles back right before winding and climbing though clumps of gorse, bracken and heather. At the next junction, turn right on a track, again signed with the North Wales Path sign. This gives glimpses of the rooftops of the coastal village of Dwygyfylchi.

At GR 750765 follow a path climbing south accompanied by wooden electricity pylons. Once over a ladder stile in a wall, turn sharp left, ignoring a path descending towards the fields and forest above Fairy Glen. The stony track passes a shallow pool, which may be dry in summer. On reaching the ridge, climb right on a narrow path to the cairned top of Maen Esgob. Descend the other side into a narrow grassy defile. The lake shown on the map, Llyn y Wrach, is out of sight from this path but a short detour right will bring it into view – it's a nice place for a refreshment break.

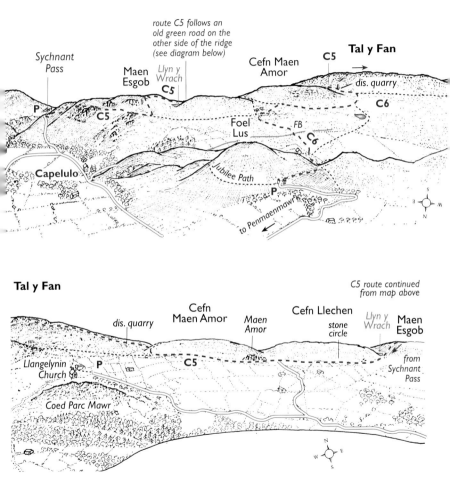

route C5 follows an old green road on the other side of the ridge (see diagram below)

Sychnant Pass

Maen Esgob

Llyn y Wrach

C5

Cefn Maen Amor

C5

Tal y Fan

dis. quarry

C6

P

C5

Foel Lus

FB

C6

Capelulo

Jubilee Path

P

to Penmaenmawr

Tal y Fan

C5 route continued from map above

dis. quarry

Cefn Maen Amor

Maen Amor

Cefn Llechen

stone circle

Llyn y Wrach

Maen Esgob

Llangelynin Church

P

C5

from Sychnant Pass

Coed Parc Mawr

39

The route veers left (south-east) to follow a grassy wallside track traversing the east side of Cefn Llechen, where you should see the remains of a stone circle. The track continues alongside this intake wall past the ruined farmhouses of Tyddyn-grasod. It rounds the east side of Cefn Maen Amor. By now Tal y Fan is dominant on the skyline ahead, as are the slate-heaps of some quarries on its north slopes. Leave the track you're on for a left turn along the quarry track.

Pass the quarry on the left and climb the pathless grass slopes to the eastern end of Tal y Fan's ridge, where a splendid undulating course leads to the summit trig point.

Above: Tal y Fan slate quarry.

Route C6
Penmaenmawr

Another long but pleasant route

Start: Car park, top of Mountain Road, Penmaenmawr (GR: SH 731759)
Distance: 3 miles/5 km
Height gain: 1280ft/390m
Time: 1½–2 hours

From the car park go through the tall stone-built gateposts on to a stony track that heads for the coastal ridge. Follow the signs for Langelynin, keeping Ty'n-y-fridd farm to the left. Go over the ladder stile on the right-hand side of the field before turning left once again on the North Wales Path to cross the Afon Gyrach on a little footbridge. The path follows the right perimeter of more fields before climbing towards the ridge north of Cefn Maen Amor.

Keep to the left of the quarry then climb the crag-punctuated slopes leading to Tal y Fan's long ridge. Beyond the enclosures turn half-right off the path to meet the marked track at GR 740747. Turn right along this track, which skirts Cefn Maen Amor and passes above an old reservoir before arcing left beneath Tal y Fan's north flanks. Leave the track for another track climbing south to a disused slate quarry. Keep to the left of the quarry then climb the craggy slopes leading to Tal y Fan's long ridge.

Above: Crossing the Afon Gyrach with Foel Lus on the horizon.

Route C7

Nant-y-coed and Foel Lwyd

A walk through delightful woodland,
*   followed by a climb over wild moorland*

Start: Nant y Coed lower car park
   (GR: SH 695739)

Distance: 3 miles/5km

Height gain: 520m (1700ft)

Time: 2 hours

An early 20th-century tourist poster described Nant y Coed as 'the loveliest sylvan rock and river scenery in Wales'. The dashing stream is shaded by beautiful deciduous woodland of alder, ash, oak and sycamore. In spring and early summer bluebells will be abundant and you'll also see wood sorrel and wood anemone.

Go through the gate beyond the car park and follow a stony path through the woods and alongside the north bank of the stream. Take the left fork, which passes the pond, then cross the river using the stepping stones. More stepping stones are used to cross a side stream before the path climbs to a second car park.

A signed path continues up the valley. Cross a footbridge over the stream and follow the waymarks, which guide you up zigzags and across a complex of criss-crossing tracks. On reaching the open moor, the route continues as a grooved, rush-filled track before deteriorating into sheep tracks through gorse bushes. Keep roughly parallel to the stream, now known as the Afon Ddu, and aim for Bwlch y Ddeufaen (pass of the two stones), where electricity pylons straddle the skyline hills.

On reaching the pass, turn left on a little path that climbs the steep, rocky slopes to the summit of Foel Lwyd, before descending to a shallow moorland saddle, where you climb back up again to the even rockier summit of Tal y Fan.

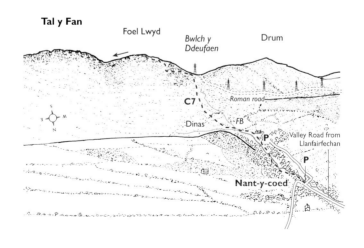

Above: Climbing Tal y Fan.

Route C8
Rowen and Coed Parc Mawr
A pleasant journey through history
Start: Rowen car park to right off main road
through village (GR: SH 759725)
Distance: 3¼ miles/6km
Height gain: 560m (1840ft)
Time: 2½ hours

From the car park, turn right up the road passing charming cottages and the village pub. Turn right along the lane signposted to the youth hostel then right again at the next junction to pass Coed Mawr Hall to the crossroads near Tyddyn Mawr farm. Turn left uphill here then right through a gate at the end to gain access to Coed Parc Mawr, a fine wooded slope managed by the Woodland Trust. Follow the winding path up to the top of the woods and continue on an enclosed track that climbs to the ancient church at Llangelynin.

Set in splendid mountain isolation high above the Conwy Valley, the rugged little church dedicated to 7th-century Celtic missionary Celynin has roots in the 12th century, although most of the current building dates from the 15th century. In the corner of the churchyard among scattered gravestones lies Ffynnon Gelynin, a holy well whose water is said to have healing powers for sick children. In times when these hillsides were more populated there was an inn next to the church. Right next to that was a cock-fighting pit. The population was dispersed following the enclosure of the land by major landowners, and the church is believed to have been demolished in the 18th century.

Continue along the track, which passes to the left of Garnedd-wen farm and arcs left behind the craggy knoll of Craig Celynin. Here the track runs alongside a stone wall to reach the remains of an Iron Age fort, Caer Bach (GR 744730), which has a large ditch and rampart on the north side and a ring of stones encircling a large white boulder. Here you should break off from the track and climb the hillside to the right, following a shallow grassy hollow to the right of the crags. This will emerge on the ridge close to a wall corner. Turn left and follow the wall along the craggy, undulating ridge to the trig point on Tal y Fan's summit.

Left: Tal y Fan from the Roman Road near Bwlch y Ddeufaen.

Route C9
Rowen and the Roman Road

A simple if unspectacular route

Start: Rowen car park to right off main road through village (GR: SH 759725)

Distance: 3 miles/6km

Height gain: 520m (1700ft)

Time: 2 hours

Follow Route C8 past the village pub and right along the lane signposted to the youth hostel but this time keep straight on at the next junction. The cul-de-sac lane has a sting in its tail as it climbs very steeply from some woods to the youth hostel where the tarmac ends. The stony track that now continues in its place is the old Roman highway that linked their forts at Caerhun, in the Conwy Valley, and Segontium at Caernarfon.

It climbs more easily at the foot of Tal y Fan then rejoins a tarred lane just beyond Cae Goch farm. After going a few yards along the road turn right to climb the ladder stile marking the start of a pleasant path climbing the gorse-scattered lower slopes of the hill. The waymarked path aims for the gap between Foel Lwyd (left) and Tal y Fan (right). Higher up it crosses a ladder stile in a wall to the right before climbing through heather to the ridge. Here, go over another ladder stile before climbing up the steep rocky slope to reach Tal y Fan's summit.

Other route options

The North Wales Path from Nant-y-coed, Llanfairfechan, could be used before taking the marked footpath south of Moelfre to the pass between Foel Lwyd and Tal y Fan. There are also several route variations from Hendryd village above the Conwy Valley.

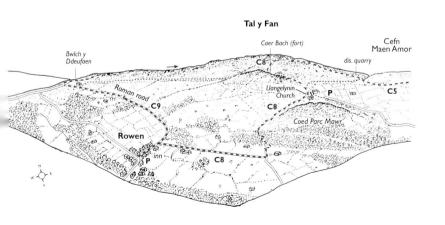

RIDGE ROUTE

Foel Lwyd

Distance: 2–3 miles/1km
Height gain: 210ft/65m
Time: ½ hour

The ridge fence/wall acts a guide all the way. The path clambers south-westwards down boulders to a col between the two peaks. A trek westwards across bilberry and heather leads gently to Foel Lwyd's summit.

Below: Tal y Fan seen from the stone circle on Moelfre.

Drum, pronounced 'drim', means simply ridge, and it's a gracefully arced, largely grassy summit lying on the main Carneddau ridge just north of Foel-fras, the most northerly of Wales's 3000ft peaks. If you're looking for the spectacular, Drum's not your place: if you're looking for great crags and rocky tors, they're not here. The mountain is just that little bit too near to Foel-fras and the more majestic Llwytmor, which lies across Cwm Anafon, to be anything other than a staging post on the way to greater things, usually the long ridge trek from Bwlch y Ddeufaen or Aber to Carnedd Llewelyn.

There's a stony vehicle track leading to the summit, which is more correctly known as Carnedd Penyborth-goch, referring to the cairn, hollowed out to form a wind shelter. The shelter is part of a near 60ft/18m Bronze Age platform or ceremonial site, one of many in the region. There's another one close by on the summit of Carnedd y Ddelw.

Although it doesn't have an ice-sculpted cwm or a tarn to call its own, Drum does overlook the deep valley of the Anafon, which has a small reservoir of the same name. It's also the highest point of an east–west ridge, which it throws out towards Tal-y-bont in the Conwy Valley. So Drum offers a great lunch stop, but you'll be itching to continue along the peaty ridge path to those 3000ers on the skyline.

ight: A cloud nversion creeps ver Foel-fras and lyn Anafon as en from Drum.

Route C10

Aber

An easy route on a vehicle track

Start: Small car park at the road-end above
    Bont Newydd (GR: SH 676716)

Distance: 3 miles/5km

Height gain: 1950ft/595m

Time: 1½ hours

From the car park take the track heading north towards the electricity pylons, where it swings right to skirt the grass slopes of Foel Dduarth and Foel-ganol. Anglesey and the surf of Conwy Bay dominate the views from here, for the surrounding hill slopes are rather stark and not enhanced by the three rows of pylons.

On reaching the crossroads south of Garreg Fawr's stony summit plateau, take the track on the right, which rounds the east flank of Yr Orsedd before straddling the ridge at Pen Bryn-du. Here you get your first big view of the day – into Cwm Anafon, whose small tarn-like reservoir lies ringed by the steep-sided, rock-scattered peaks of Llwytmor and Foel-fras. The track keeps to the Anafon side of the ridge before climbing to the top of Drum, but leave it now (at the ridge crossing) to follow the grassy crest over Carnedd y Ddelw before continuing to Drum's summit cairn.

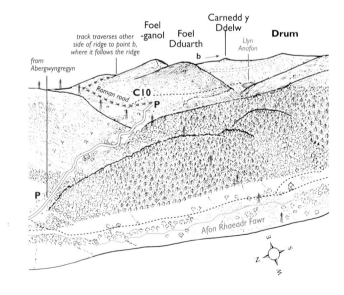

Route C11
Cwm Dulyn and Pen y Castell

*A seldom-used route visiting two secretive
    crag-ringed tarns*
Start: Bwlch y Gaer (GR: SH 747696)
Distance: 3 miles/5km
Height gain: 1575ft/480m
Time: 1½–2 hours

Follow the westbound track from the road-end, taking the upper right fork before Bwlch y Gaer farm. The old packhorse route which once linked the Conwy Valley with the coast at Bangor climbs the south slopes of Penygadair high above the desolate fields of Cwm Dulyn. Beyond a third gate in the track you'll notice a gate in the fence to the right. Go though this to gain a faint path climbing westwards up the sullen south flanks of Pen y Castell (castle hill). In the upper reaches the path nears a drystone wall. For those who wish to climb to Pen y Castell's summit, the best place to do so is from a wall corner at GR 719689, where it is a short sharp step there and back over rock and heather. Otherwise go over the stile to the right of the wall corner and continue the climb across marshy moorland all the way to the summit of Drum.

Other route options
The quickest route of ascent is from the high car park at the end of the Bwlch y Ddeufaen road (accessed from Tal-y-bont or Rowen). At the pass you just climb south-west up the steep but dull ridge of Drosgl, joining Route C10 on Carnedd y Ddelw. Alternatively there's the track to Llyn Anafon, but that leaves a 1000ft slog up Drum's steep west flank.

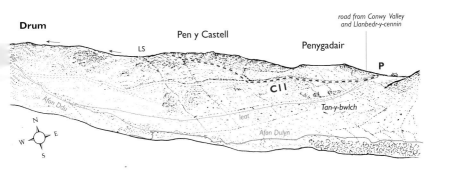

RIDGE ROUTES

Pen y Castell

Distance: 1 mile/1.5km
Height gain: 100ft/30m
Time: ¼ hour

A straightforward, generally downhill, route by a fence and over marshy grass slopes. Beyond a ladder stile near the col there's a short pathless climb to the rocky summit.

Foel-fras

Distance: 1¼ miles/2km
Height gain: 720ft/220m
Time: ¾ hour

A simple stride over a peat-and-grass rid[ge] overlooking the upper Cwm Anafon. Ju[st] follow the ridge fence.

Foel-fras, whose name means the prominent bare hill, is a gently domed grassy giant, the most northerly of the Welsh 3000-foot summits. Little more than a swelling in the northern ridges, it's only blessed with some sparse crags above Cwm Anafon and a rash of boulders on the summit. Perhaps the mountain's best feature, Craig y Dulyn, is shared with neighbouring Foel Grach and Garnedd Uchaf. Here, broken cliffs form a tight ring around the cwm of the Dulyn Reservoir, an attractive tarn which was enlarged by the building of a dam in 1881 in order to supply the growing holiday resort of Llandudno with water.

Opposite: Walkers descending Pen y Castell. Below: Llyn Anafon and the North Wales coast seen from the slopes of Foel-fras.

Foel-fras lies at the head of three deep, lonely valleys – those of the Afon Goch, the Anafon and the Dulyn. On most long routes it offers either the first or last highlight on a pleasing ridge walk – but it's rarely the high point of the day. Like Tal y Fan in the north, this mountain is known better for its horizons than its environs. The view north across the Anafon lake and across its scything valley to Puffin Island and Anglesey is particularly memorable, as is the the one east to the Conwy Valley, its sandbars and little pastured hills. I once camped here on a settled spring evening and was rewarded by a crystal-clear view under darkening skies, with orange streetlights highlighting the whole of North Wales and the Wirral coastline.

There's something else I've noticed, too: standing on the summit on a clear day I could swear that Foel-fras is higher than neighbouring Foel Grach, even though the map-maker says it isn't so.

Route C12
Aber Falls

A long trek that would be difficult in hill fog
Start: Forestry car park (GR: SH 663719)
Distance: 5 miles/8km
Height gain: 2950ft/900m
Time: 3–3½ hours

From the car park head back down the road before turning left through a gate to gain a track through the beautiful, partially wooded glen of the Afon Rhaeadr-fawr. After passing under the electricity pylons, watch out for a signed path forking left. This passes to the left of the Nant Rhaeadr information centre and follows the edge of a conifer-clad slope. Eventually the path enters the plantation before emerging on a vast scree slope to the left of Aber Falls, which can be seen tumbling down a crag-face to the valley below.

A narrow path crosses the screes. Walkers wandering from the falls and grazing sheep have eroded the screes in places and added extra paths. The correct path makes its exit from the screes just above a fence. The now rather exciting path clambers over the rocks to the left of the falls. There's one rather wet and slippery rock to negotiate before entering into the wild world of the Afon Goch river, which cuts a deep bouldery trench through the mountainsides before feeding the falls.

A narrow path now traces the bounding river with the serrated, craggy cone of Bera Mawr peeping over stony hillslopes. Llwytmor soon comes into view and the river scenery gets more spectacular as the torrent of white water thrashes through rocky gorges in a series of attractive waterfalls. The rocks get sparser as the head of the valley looms. The path soon gives up the ghost, so you just

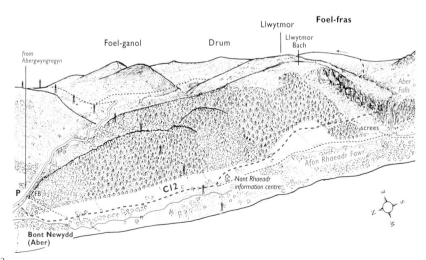

head south to the shallow dip between Foel-fras and Garnedd Uchaf. The hard work has been done and you are rewarded by a spectacular view of Yr Elen's crags and screes backed up by the huge massif of Carnedd Llewelyn.

Turn left along the ridge path over a peaty grass ridge to the bouldered summit of Foel-fras.

Below: Crossing the great screes next to Aber Falls. Beyond these an exciting ledge path leads to one of Snowdonia's loneliest hanging valleys, that of the Afon Goch, which bites deep into the high Carneddau peaks.

Route C13
Bwlch y Gaer
A rather sombre route
Start: Bwlch y Gaer (GR: SH 747696)
Distance: 4½ miles/7km
Height gain: 1900ft/580m
Time: 3 hours

Cwm Dulyn is a longish, rather sulky place for much of its length. From the small car-parking area at the road-end, take the upper right fork track, an old packhorse trail, which traverses the sides of Penygadair and the rock-fringed Pen y Castell. The cart track ends on reaching the banks of the Afon Ddu below Cwm Bychan. Cross the stile here and follow a faint path climbing the grassy east flanks of Foel-fras. The route virtually disappears, leaving the walker to plot his or her own course WSW to the saddle between Garnedd Uchaf and Foel-fras. On reaching the saddle turn right to follow the ridge fence to Foel-fras.

Other route options
Perhaps the easiest way to Foel-fras would be to follow Route C10 to Drum and continue south along the ridge. This would work well as a circular with Route C11.

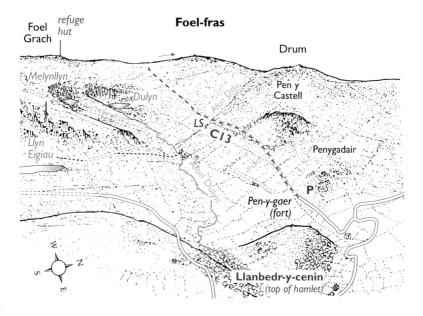

RIDGE ROUTES

Drum

Distance: 1¼ miles/2km
Height gain: 130ft/40m
Time: ¾ hour

A ridge fence leads all the way over a peaty grass ridge.

Llwytmor

Distance: 1 mile/1.5km
Height gain: 250ft/75m
Time: ¾ hour

Not easy in hill fog, because there is no real path. A broad grass slope descends to Llwytmor's rocky top.

Garnedd Uchaf (Carnedd Gwenllian)

Distance: 1 mile/1.5km
Height gain: 100ft/30m
Time: ½ hour

A very easy stride, following a ridge fence at first. This descends left halfway down the broad ridge slopes of Foel-fras and ceases to be of use. The path rounds the rim of Cwm yr Afon Goch. Take the right fork path at the grassy col – the left fork heads directly for Foel Grach and bypasses Garnedd Uchaf – then the climb to Garnedd Uchaf's rock outcrops involves little ascent or effort.

Below: Mist over Cwm Yr Afon-goch.

GARNEDD UCHAF (CARNEDD GWENLLIAN)

The fact that Garnedd Uchaf has recently been added to the list of 3000ers has saved it from anonymity. In reality it is only one of several rocky tors at the heart of the Carneddau. Geographically it is the high point of a long ridge declining westwards down to Bethesda and overlooking the desolate marshy hollow of Cwm Caseg. One look at the map tells you that several public footpaths aim for its summit then, at the last minute, steer a course round the sides.

Controversially, in late September 2009, the Ordnance Survey, at the request of the Princess Gwenllian Society, agreed to add the name Carnedd Gwenllian after the daughter of Llewelyn, Prince of Wales. They insist, however, that the name Garnedd Uchaf will also remain on the maps for mountain rescue purposes.

Garnedd Uchaf (the upper cairn) does have a good rocky top, and it's a good viewing platform lying at the head of the wild glen of the Afon Goch. In the last 20 years, the peak baggers among us have forged a clear course to its summit, and you'll seldom be alone here. Long live imperial measurement!

Right: On the rocky summit of Garnedd Uchaf looking to Carnedd Llewelyn and Yr Elen (photograph by Roy Clayton).

RIDGE ROUTES

Foel-fras
Distance: 1 mile/1.5km
Height gain: 165ft/50m
Time: ½ hour

Head north-east across stony ground to the grassy col at the head of Cwm yr Afon Goch before climbing a peaty ridge towards the rounded top of Foel-fras. A fence and wall accompany the path in the later stages, leading all the way to the summit trig point.

Bera Bach
Distance: 1 mile/1.5km
Height gain: 250ft/10m
Time: ¾ hour

Descend west along the stony ridge before scrambling up the rocks to Bera Bach's summit.

Above: Llwytmor Bach and the great screes that flank the Aber Falls.

One writer described Llwytmor as an insignificant grassy lump lying on a broad ridge extending north from Foel-fras; another wrote that its high summit plateau was not without appeal and that it conjured up images of a lost world, in its sheer abandon and isolation. One thing's for sure – Llwytmor is a brute of a hill, a Rocky Marciano or a Mike Tyson, broad in the beam, low on height (it doesn't make 3000 feet like many of its neighbours).

Seen from the west, tops like Moel Wnion make the mountain look quite distinctive, but unless you cheat and do a there-and-back ridge walk from Foel-fras, the ascent will rob you of your energy. You may come across the wreckage of a World War II Blackburn Botha, whose crew of four were killed when it crashed into the mountain on 21 July 1942.

Llwytmor lies between the valleys of Ana-fon and the Afon Goch above the Aber Falls, and it is from here the usual ascents begin. I say usual but unless it's a fine bank holiday it's unlikely you'll see anybody else anywhere near the summit. This enhances its lonely wilderness appeal, and although Foel-fras blocks out its views of the bigger mountains, the empty uncultivated mountainscapes of the Afon Goch, the serrated peaks of Bera Mawr, Bera Bach and Drosgl, and the sea-scapes towards the Isle of Anglesey make this a very pleasant place to rest and recuperate before heading back down to Aber.

Route C14

Aber Falls and the Afon Goch

A long, strenuous but stimulating route

Start: Forestry car park (GR: SH 663719)

Distance: 5 miles/5km

Height gain: 2560ft/780m

Time: 3 hours

After heading back down the lane for a few paces turn left through a gate and follow the wide path through the glen of the Afon Rhaeadr. This is now part of the Coedydd Aber National Nature Reserve, set up in 1975 as a fine example of broadleaved woodland.

On your left are the dark spruce woods of Forestry Enterprise, but in the more swampy ground to the right you'll see alders. In spring the scene will be splashed by the colourful blooms of marsh marigold. Possibly the woods and meadows will be also echoing to the calls of wood warblers, redstarts and pied flycatchers.

After passing under electricity pylons take the signed left fork, which passes to the left of the Nant Rhaeadr information centre, eventually to enter the conifer forest. Over the stile at the other end of the plantation, the path is confronted by a vast scree slope left of the Aber Falls, whose white waters plunge hundreds of feet down cliffs of quartz-streaked Cambrian granophyre. The longest single drop is 115ft/35m. Scrub birch trees eke out an existence high on the rock-ledges, as do liverworts, rare mosses and lichens, primroses and anemones.

Follow a narrow path traversing the screes to reach the cliffs left of the falls. A path now winds over the rocks. There is one short but tricky section where a spring makes the rock surface a little slippery. Over the cliffs the

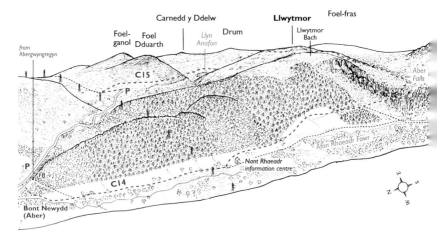

path enters the wild cwm of the Afon Goch at the top of the falls. It follows the east bank of the lively river, with the ragged cone of Bera Mawr peeping over a corridor of grass and boulder. Llwytmor finally appears on the left.

You could strike out for it almost any-where, though the left sides of the cwm are very steep at first. The best place is just beyond the gorge at the foot of Bera Mawr's rocky eastern arm, where there is a series of waterfalls. From here it's a steep slog on grass slopes peppered with rocky bluffs and boul-ders. Keep to the left of the main spiky crags and you'll come to the summit plateau, pass-ing the huge hollowed-out cairn before reaching the smaller summit cairn.

Below: The lovely Afon Goch stream above Aber Falls.

Route C15
Cwm Anafon

Pleasant, easy-paced walk with a sting in the tail

Start: Small car park at the road-end above Bont Newydd (GR: SH 676716)
Distance: 3¼ miles/6km
Height gain: 2070ft/630m
Time: 2½ hours

From the little car-parking area, double back left on a stony northbound track. On reaching the electricity pylons double back again right on another track, which traverses the west side of Foel Dduarth before entering Cwm Anafon, a pleasant valley with meadows by a tree-lined riverbank. The situation gets wilder as gorse and bracken take over and Foel-fras, Drum and Llwytmor close in. The track ends at the Llyn Anafon reservoir. Now the hard work begins. Round the lake on the left and climb the steep rock-studded slopes to the col between Foel-fras and Lwytmor. From here it's a simple ridge walk to the summit.

RIDGE ROUTE

Foel-fras
Distance: 1 mile/1.5km
Height gain: 560ft/170m
Time: ½ hour

Descend south-east to a broad marshy col before climbing pathless grassy slopes to the ridge wall and trig point on Foel-fras.

With a name that means the big and the little pyramids, Bera Mawr and Bera Bach sound promising, and so they are. Bera Mawr is a fine peak with serrated craggy outlines. When seen from Aber it's an imposing sight and it loses no appeal on closer approaches through the rugged mountain glen of the Afon Goch.

Like its neighbour Llwytmor, there are no easy direct ascents to Bera Mawr: no paths climb either east or west flanks, and the cliffs around the northern flanks offer no secretive walkers' routes either. This may be off-putting to the casual walker but somehow adds appeal to the mountain connoisseur, who would delight at the ledge path around the Aber Falls before the climb from the Afon Goch among the spiky tors which proliferate on the high slopes.

A rather marshy ridge leads to the jagged crags and boulders of Bera Bach, some half a mile/800m away, and it soon becomes obvious that Bera Mawr is every bit the superior of the two peaks. Bera Bach is on the highway ridge from Bethesda to the main Carneddau ridge; it's well-walked and you've lost the feeling of remoteness completely. Yet Bera Bach should be called Bera Mawr, for it's 42ft/13m higher.

Opposite: The summit rocks of Bera Mawr.
Below: Bera Bach from Cwm Caseg.

Route C16

Aber Falls and the Afon Goch

A strenuous but attractive walk of contrasts

Start: Forestry car park (GR: SH 663719)

Distance: 5 miles/8km

Height gain: 2950ft/900m

Time: 3–3½ hours

From the forestry car park head back down the road before turning left through a gate to gain a track into the glen of the Afon Rhaeadr-fawr. After passing under the electricity pylons, a signed path forking left follows the edge of the conifer-clad slopes. The path enters the plantation before emerging on a vast scree slope to the left of Aber Falls, whose torrents can be seen tumbling down tree-hung cliffs.

A narrow path crosses the screes to make its exit just above a fence. Then an exciting ledge path winds around the cliffs to reach the top of the falls – there's just one greasy rock to negotiate en route. The path – and the inner sanctum of the Afon Goch's hanging valley where it traces the stream's east bank – and the rugged cone of Bera Mawr come into view to the right. The river is usually cross-able above a series of waterfalls just over a

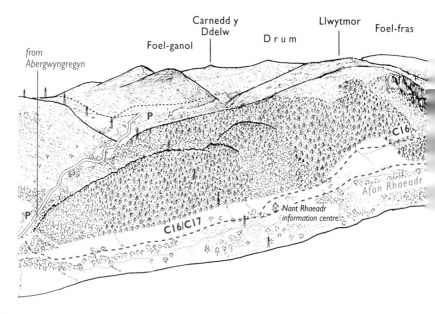

mile along the valley. During dry summers you can cross earlier to gain the rocks of the sporty northern spur.

From above the falls climb south-west over rocky ground – sometimes the route offers a little scrambling although it is avoidable. However, to reach the narrow rocky crest which is the very highest point, you've no alternative but to get your hands on the rock. The continuation to Bera Bach is by way of a boulder-hopping descent, followed by a straightforward but damp half-mile of ridge and a short scramble to the spiky summit.

Route C17
Aber, the Afon Gam and North-West Ridge
A strenuous but scenically attractive walk
Start: Forestry car park (GR: SH 663719)
Distance: 3¼ miles/6km
Height gain: 1740ft/530m
Time: 2½ hours

As in Route C16, turn left through a gate to gain a track into the glen of the Afon Rhaeadr-fawr but this time stay with the signed lower path to the falls, keeping to the right of the Nant Rhaeadr information centre. On the

Below: Fording Afon Gam.

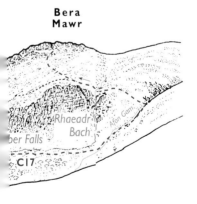

approach to the falls, turn right on a path that skirts the foot of the cliffs, crossing beneath the Rhaeadr Bach Falls on a wooden footbridge.

At the next stream, the Afon Gam, turn left over a ladder stile and follow a narrow path over the stream before climbing a spur of bracken and grass. The path is joined from the right by one that has traversed the mid slopes of Moel Wnion; together they ford the Gam beneath low gritty cliffs.

Follow a clear path raking left up hill slopes of the far bank. The path selects a delightful panoramic route towards the crags above the Rhaeadr Bach Falls. There are splendid views down Aber's Glen towards Anglesey, Puffin Island and the Great Orme. Eventually the path descends to cross the Afon Rhaeadr Bach. Beyond this it becomes fairly faint as it climbs bilberry slopes.

Look out for a sheepfold on slopes above on the right to locate the easier ground of a grassy chase through the bilberry – there are no traces of a path. Climb this towards Bera Mawr's north-west spur. Follow the crest of the spur over rough slopes of grass, bilberry and a little heather. As the gradient eases, Bera Mawr's serrated summit ridge comes into view. This route makes a beeline for the centre of the summit massif, where you'll see a grassy rake leading to the skyline. This leaves you a short bouldery climb before scrambling to the rocky summit crest.

Opposite: Aber Falls and Bera Mawr.

Route C18
Bethesda

The easiest way – a pleasant ridge walk

Start: Bethesda's riverside car park
  (GR: SH 622668)
Distance: 4½ miles/7km
Height gain: 2260ft/690m
Time: 3 hours

Although you could probably find a parking place somewhere on the streets of Gerlan, I've started the route description from the riverside car park in Bethesda's town centre. From here head back to the High Street and turn right. Turn left on the street signed to Pen y Bryn School before taking the right fork, Pant Glas Road, which is signed 'to Gerlan'.

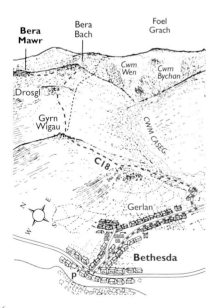

At the next crossroads go straight ahead along Ffordd Gerlan, which is Gerlan's main street. Turn left along the lane at the end of the houses and follow it up the hillside past several cottages. The lane degenerates into a cart track which terminates at a gate (GR 639665) at the south-western foot of Gyrn Wigau, the grassy knuckle of one of the Carneddau's great ridges.

Turn right along the grass track until the first slight bend in the track, where you head north-eastwards across grass and bracken-clad slopes, aiming for a ladder stile on the skyline. Once on the ridge, the sombre scenes of the Caseg valley's wet and rushy pastures are left behind. They are now dominated by the distinctive shale and rock peak of Yr Elen (hill of the fawn) and the savage cliffs of Ysgolion Duon (the Black Ladders).

The bracken and bilberry of the lower ridge gives way to grass on the approach to Drosgl. The path divides just short of its summit: the upper one stays on the ridge while the lower one rakes across the high southern slopes. Either will lead to the saddle between Drosgl and the next peak, Bera Bach, where you climb the summit crags Bera Mawr lies across damp moorland but it's an easy slightly downhill trek before scampering up to the summit.

Above: Drosgl, Bera Bach and Garnedd Uchaf from Gyrn Wigau.

RIDGE ROUTES (from Bera Bach)

Garnedd Uchaf (Carnedd Gwenllian)

Distance: 1 mile/1.5km
Height gain: 395ft/120m
Time: ¼ hour

After descending Bera Bach's rocky slopes stay on the highest ground, passing over 'r Aryg to Garnedd Uchaf's summit outcrops.

Drosgl

Distance: ⅔ mile/1km
Height gain: 260ft/80m
Time: ½ hour

After clambering eastwards down craggy slopes, continue across a grass ridge, taking care not to be lured on to a wider path on the left, which bypasses Drosgl. Keep to the highest ground.

Above: Gyrn and Drosgl seen from Route C19 rounding Moel Faban.

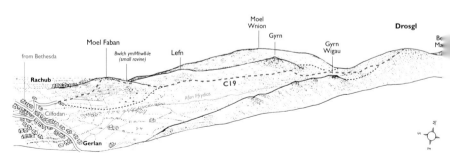

Like Bera Mawr and Moel Wnion, Drosgl feels remote from modern civilization – something that is so typical of the Northern Carneddau. The wild grassy col between Moel Wnion and Drosgl, often grazed by wild Carneddau ponies, is as uncultivated as Wales gets, with no walls or fences in sight. With so few visitors there is seldom more than the sound of the breeze and your own breathing to hear; or maybe the occasional whinnying of those ponies as they gallop across the hillsides.

There's no great mountain form to Drosgl: it's just a huge grassy dome in a long ridge connecting Bethesda and the Carneddau spine at Garnedd Uchaf. Most walkers who set foot on Drosgl follow the wide path traversing its southern flanks, high above Cwm Caseg. They're bound for the more spectacular environs of Carnedd Llewelyn, the Black Ladders and Carnedd Dafydd. But they'll miss out on the solitude, they'll not see the huge summit cairn which dates back to the Bronze Age, and they'll miss the tremendous view northeastwards to the crags of Bera Bach and Bera Mawr, the latter rising like a castle on the dark, windswept moorland horizon. The trouble with Drosgl is that there's always something else to explore.

Route C19
From Bethesda
A route through ancient history
Start: Bethesda car park (GR: SH 622668)
Distance: 4 miles/6km
Height gain: 2070ft/630m
Time: 2½ hours

From Betheda's riverside car park, turn right along the main street, then left to follow Penbryn Road to its junction with Ffordd Frydlas. Turn left here. Double back right along Ffordd Carnedd, then left up the winding Cilfodan Terrace. Beyond Tan-y-Foel Cottages the lane becomes a track climbing towards the rough fellsides beneath Moel Faban.

As the track swings right towards a whitewashed farmhouse, keep straight ahead to a gate in the intake wall. Once through the gate follow a grassy track on the right. This skirts Moel Faban and stays with the wall until a wall corner. Here the path goes straight on towards the open hillside, with the angular summit of Gyrn straight ahead and the Gyrn Wigau ridge to the right. Stay with the track over low ground beneath Lefn before swinging first right then left to round Y Gyrn to reach a wild moorland col between the smooth rounded massifs of Moel Wnion and Drosgl. There are often Carneddau ponies grazing here.

A clearly discernable path climbs southeast over the right shoulder of Drosgl to join the ridge. Here you look down on the deep chasm of Cwm Caseg towards Yr Elen and Carnedd Llewelyn. On reaching the ridge it is of no further use as it continues along the south side of the hill. Stay with the ridge to climb to Drosgl's stony summit and its huge cairn.

Other route options

Due to Drosgl's position, other options are infinite. More often than not Drosgl will be part of an itinerary to higher tops. There are several routes from Abergwyngregyn (often known as just Aber). One goes through the glen to the base of the falls before turning right and climbing by the Afon Gam (see Route C19 to Moel Wnion). This would lead to the moorland col in Route C18. Another good route begins at Bronydd Isaf (GR 625705) and climbs between Moel Wnion and Y Gyrn to the same col.

RIDGE ROUTES

Bera Bach
Distance: 2–3 miles/1km
Height gain: 130ft/40m
Time: ½ hour

From Drosgl's domed summit the grass and stone ridge narrows. At the col make sure you don't get lured on to the main Cwm Caseg path which bypasses all the tops. Stay on the highest ground heading for the rock tors of Bera Bach, clambering over those rocks to reach the summit.

Moel Wnion
Distance: 1¼ miles/3km
Height gain: 360ft/110m
Time: 1 hour

Follow Drosgl's south-west spur towards Gyrn Wigau, but watch for the path coming in from the left. Where you join it, descend NNW to a wild moorland col with the huge domed summit of Moel Wnion directly ahead. At the col head for the gap between Moel Wnion and the miniature rocky pyramid that is Y Gyrn. From here the faintest of paths climbs grass slopes to the cairn and wind shelter on Moel Wnion's summit.

Opposite: The dome of Moel Wnion rises above verdant coastal pastures.

Moel Wnion is the north-eastern outlier of the Carneddau, a smooth-profiled hill overlooking Bangor, the expansive Lavan Sands and the Isle of Anglesey. Although it possesses considerable girth, Moel Wnion lacks the magic 2000ft contour, which more often than not means it misses being added to the list-tickers' itineraries. Luckily, this means that there are no eroded paths anywhere near the hill and lends a sense of tranquillity and spaciousness to the place.

The huge grassy summit dome is capped by a trig point and wind shelter. Surprisingly for a hill on the edge of the range, the views are excellent, including unfamiliar angles on familiar peaks. I found the view north-eastwards across the bleak moorland shoulder of Drosgl absolutely fascinating, with my eyes being drawn through the lonely cwms of Anafon and the Afon Goch, over the spiky rocks of Lwytmor and Bera Mawr, through to the giants of the Southern Carneddau.

While Moel Wnion is a bit of a frump, the peak of Gyrn, which lies on its southern shoulder, is a bouldery cone of diminutive girth. It has a a very elaborate sheepfold at its foot and a huge, hollowed-out cairn on the summit. For those who are interested in ancient history, Moel Wnion's eastern slopes and the area around Gyrn are scattered with relics of prehistoric and medieval settlement – round houses, cairns, rectangular huts and terraced field systems.

Route C20
Abergwyngregyn

Wonderful views of the Aber Falls and its glen

Start: Car park entrance to Aber village (GR: SH 655727)
Distance: 2¼ miles/4.5km
Height gain: 1800ft/550m
Time: 2 hours

From the car park head back along the road towards the Aber Falls Inn, turn left along the signed footpath then follow the lane through the village past the Hen Felin (old mill) café . Take the second signed footpath on the right, a narrow path beyond a small gate. This rakes spectacularly across steep grass slopes with superb views back to the village and coastline. Note the mound of a motte-and-bailey castle at the back of the village. This is said to have been home to Llewelyn the Great, 13th-century Prince of Wales.

On reaching a conifer wood turn left along a wide track and follow it along the rim of the Afon Rhaeadr-fawr glen. At another conifer plantation (GR 661717), leave the track for a right of way (non-existent on the ground) which climbs SSW across high pastures. There's a ladder stile to be crossed in the fence ahead as you go under rows of electricity pylons.

By maintaining this direction, you'll reach a gate in the intake wall by some sheepfolds. The faint path you'll see is of no use so it's better just to climb the moor keeping the crags of Cras to the right. Eventually you meet and turn left along a clear path heading southwards on the high slopes of Moel Wnion. The views to the Aber Falls and the peaks of Bera Mawr and Llwytmor make the effort of the day worthwhile.

Where the path levels out above the hollow of the Afon Gam, leave it and climb right to Moel Wnion's summit.

Opposite: Climbing away from Abergwyngregyn on Route C20.

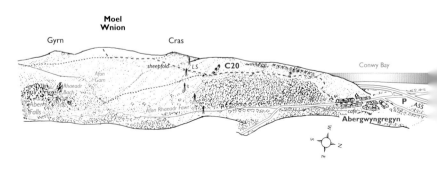

Route C21
Bethesda, Moel Faban and Gyrn

Starts in industrial slate mining country;
culminates with wilderness

Start: Bethesda car park (GR: SH 622668)
Distance: 3¼ miles/5km
Height gain: 1800ft/550m
Time: 2–2½ hours (ascent)

From the car park turn right along the main street then left along Penbryn Road (signed to Pen y Bryn School) to its junction with Ffordd Frydlas. Here you turn left. Double back right along Ffordd Carnedd then left up the winding Cilfodan Terrace. Beyond Tan-y-Foel Cottages the lane becomes a walled track climbing to the rough hillsides beneath Moel Faban.

As the track swings right towards the whitewashed farmhouse, keep straight ahead to a gate in the intake wall which gives access to the path to Moel Faban. This whole area was occupied from the Bronze Age to medieval times, and for historians and archaeologists makes a fascinating day on its own. A good path climbs to the stony hilltop, where there are three Bronze Age burial cairns.

On reaching the last cairn, head west to the wide moorland hollow at the head of Cwm Ffrydlas, where a path rounds the east slopes of Llefn to reach the foot of Gyrn. Although it's possible to avoid Gyrn, it's better to tackle this fine little peak. Scale its easy grass slopes at first, then clamber over its upper boulder-slopes to the wind shelter on its summit. There's more of the same on the

descent as you pass to the left of the complex of sheep enclosures. Now the rounded dome of Moel Wnion lies ahead and a faint track climbs directly to the summit.

Other route options

There are many route options from the old coast road between Abergwyngregyn and Penrhyn. The easiest begins at Ty'n yr-hendre and follows a steep tarred lane to Bronydd Isaf, where a track leads up the hillsides to the moorland col between Moel Wnion and Y Gyrn. The high village of Rachub above Bethesda also gives an easy passage through quarries and ancient settlements to the northeast of Gyrn, before joining the previously mentioned Ty'n yr-hendre path east of Moel Wnion.

RIDGE ROUTES

Drosgl

Distance: 1¼ mile/3km
Height gain: 920ft/280m
Time: 1 hour

Descend south to the col beneath the rocky peak of Gyrn, then turn right across the wide moorland col which separates the valleys of the Afon Ffrydias and the Afon Gam. Take the narrow path which can be seen raking SSE across the right shoulder of Drosgl (the domed, grassy peak ahead). On reaching the top of this shoulder, turn left to climb the grassy spur to the summit.

Above: On Gyrn summit looking south to Moel Faban.

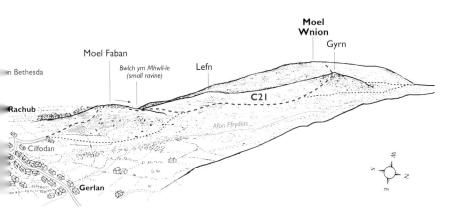

CRIMPIAU

At just 1558ft/475m, Crimpiau doesn't figure in many mountain lists, but it has to be one of Wales's best little peaks. It lies to the west of a pass between Cwm Crafnant in the north and the Llugwy valley above Capel Curig and is one of several rocky summits that rise to the twin-peaked Creigiau Gleision.

Crimpiau's name means sharp, hard edge, which is very fitting, as the peak has a nice little ridge with crags. Usually tackled from Capel Curig or Llyn Crafnant it has a distinctive, gnarled rock appearance. In most views from the beautiful Llyn Crafnant, Crimpiau, which lies at the very head of the cwm, wrestles the limelight from Gleision, for its dark rocks contrast dramatically with the green pastures beyond the lake.

Above: Looking south from the high slopes of Crimpiau towards Capel Curig (hidden) and the twin lakes of Mymbyr.

The mountain sends out a typically rocky, heather-cloaked spur south-westwards to Capel Curig, ending at Clogwyn-mawr and the famous Pinnacles (Y Pincin). Sheltered in a lonely hollow halfway along this knobbly ridge is Llyn y Coryn, a shallow pool which is an ideal place to take in the mountain view over a cup of coffee and a sandwich.

Crimpiau will not offer you epic mountain journeys, but it does provide some sporty half-day climbs. Of course it could be used as a stepping-stone to higher things such as Creigiau Gleision, but on a fine day you may never find the desire to go past its delectable summit. Wouldn't it be nice to find a rock or bed of heather on which to laze away the day with one of Snowdonia's most splendid views, that of the Glyder ridge, paraded across the Llugwy and Ogwen valleys?

Route C22
Crimpiau and Llyn Crafnant

A pleasing route from a well-loved beauty spot

Start: Llyn Crafnant car park
  (GR: SH 756618)
Distance: 2½ miles/4km
Height gain: 1050ft/320m
Time: 1½ hours

Make your way to the road-end beyond Llyn Crafnant, either by the road itself or the stony forestry tracks that run above the north-west shores of the reservoir. Follow the approach track to the climbers' hut at Blaen y Nant, beyond which the right of way turns left to cross a field. After going through a gate in the far wall, turn right on a path that becomes a green ribbon winding through bracken and

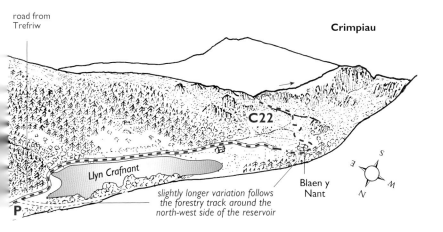

road from Trefriw

Crimpiau

C22

Llyn Crafnant

Blaen y Nant

slightly longer variation follows the forestry track around the north-west side of the reservoir

P

Above: Crimpiau at the head of Cwm Crafnant.

through gaps in cross-walls until it reaches the col at the head of the valley. Here, a narrow path on the right now tackles Crimpiau. This soon splits into two: the best one, though more of an easy scramble in places, keeps close to the Crafnant edge and offers fine views down to the lake.

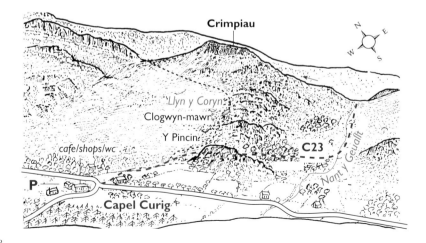

Route C23
Capel Curig and Nant y Geuallt
Another splendid half-day route
Start: Capel Curig car park behind Joe
    Brown's outdoor shop (GR: SH 720582)
Distance: 2½ miles/4km
Height gain: 950ft/290m
Time: 1½ hours

Go over a ladder stile between the war memorial and the little church of St Curig and cross a field, aiming left of the Capel Curig Pinnacles (Y Pincin). Over another ladder stile the path crosses a small stream via a slabbed bridge and, now paved, heads east across rough pastureland on the north side of the Pinnacles. Beyond an undulating section through some oak woodland and two adjacent ladder stiles, a path from the youth hostel joins in from the right.

After traversing damp moorland high above the Llugwy valley and crossing the Nant y Geuallt stream, you need to take the left of two waymarked paths. This climbs north-east, taking the walk to new heights in scenery and elevation. To your right across a flat marshy basin, the knobbly ridge of Creigiau Geuallt parades rock buttresses and outcrops studded with heather and bracken, glowing a fiery red in autumn. Crimpiau rises higher in the skyline ahead as the path nears the top of the pass. There's an expectation of seeing Llyn Crafnant but when you get to the pass you find it's round the corner out of view. Turn left and follow Route C22 up the crag and heather ridge to the summit.

Other route options
In a variation of Route C22, it is possible to climb left behind Clogwyn-mawr to reach Llyn y Coryn, where a narrow path climbs Crimpiau's heathery south-west spur to the summit.

RIDGE ROUTES

Creigiau Gleision
Distance: 1¼ miles/2km
Height gain: 1180ft/360m
Time: 1 hour

Having enjoyed the sporty ridge to Crimpiau, many want more of the same, and the continuation to Creigiau Gleision provides just that. From Crimpiau's summit, ignore the south-west-bound ridge path – that goes to Llyn y Coryn – and instead take the path descending steeply to the head of Cwm Llewesig. The descent looks much greater at first because the true col is out of view, but the path veers left through a broken-down drystone wall and all is revealed. Another steepish climb follows towards Craig Wen (the white crag). The path aims for the shoulder to the left of the biggest rock face, then angles right towards Creigiau Gleision. The clear peaty path generally keeps the rocky crests to the right until the last, when it climbs to the higher southern summit.

Though nowhere near the highest, Creigiau Gleision is the finest of the Carneddau peaks, an enthralling complex of rocky knolls, precipitous crag-faces, heathery hollows and luxuriant beds of bilberries. If you were looking for a comparison, the rugged northern Rhinog mountains would be the closest.

The mountain has two summits, the higher being the southern one. The northern top, crowned by a pile of stones, also has a tiny tarn sheltering beneath some outcrops. Some of the crags are streaked by incredible, gleaming white quartzite. On the north-west side, precipitous heather-and-scree slopes with striated crags plummet to the shores of the Cowlyd Reservoir, which is over 200ft/ 61m deep.

The view down these slopes from the summit rim has that real Alpine atmosphere, especially in swirling breeze-blown mist. To the south the flanks, rocky at first, have a steady but easier gradient and are clad with spruce and larch woodland which spreads down to the shores of the famed beauty spot, Llyn Crafnant.

To the south, the knobbly ridge continues with Craig Wen, then arcs around the head of Cwm Crafnant with the summit of Crimpiau, beyond which the lower peaks get submerged in the forests of Beddgelert.

Opposite: Looking across Creigiau Gleision's precipitous flanks to Llyn Cowlyd.
Below: Creigiau Gleision skulks behind Craig Wen when seen from the Llugwy valley near Capel Curig.

Route C24
Crafnant

An interesting route with good views of Llyn Crafnant

Start: Llyn Crafnant car park
   (GR: SH 756618)
Distance: 4 miles/6.5km
Height gain: 1870ft/570m
Time: 2½ hours

From the car park walk back along the road towards Trefriw, then take a tarred lane forking left uphill through woodland. Ignore the signed right of way at the apex of a sharp bend and continue along the lane to pass beneath a whitewashed cottage. Beyond this the lane becomes a stony one. The stone-built farmhouse of Lledwigan appears ahead, but you leave the lane for a waymarked path on the right. This zigzags up the hillside to reach a ladder stile. Over this keep straight ahead,

ignoring a path doubling back on the right. The path becomes less distinct as it threads through scattered thorn trees, but waymarkers highlight the route to another ladder stile in the intake wall.

Now a sunken track climbs across rough moors of heather and moss. There are fine views in the early stages down to Llyn Crafnant. Moel Siabod is the dominant mountain on the horizon beyond the distinctive knobbly peak of Crimpiau.

The path reaches the ridge at a ladder stile near an intersection of fences. Beyond it a narrow path veers left through the heather. Recross the ridge fence at the next ladder stile and follow the path along the ridge – it's a little drier this side. The ground steepens and the route veers right (westwards) to climb to Creigiau Gleision's lower north summit. A good path connects this to the south summit after crossing a heathery depression.

Below: Creigiau Gleision from Crimpiau.

Route C25
Coed Crafnant
A quick route but better as a descent
Start: Llyn Crafnant car park
   (GR: SH 756618)
Distance: 3½ miles/5.5km
Height gain: 1800ft/550m
Time: 2 hours

Turn right out of the car park and follow the road to Llyn Crafnant's northern tip. Here turn right following the stony forestry track alongside the west shores. Take the upper right fork and follow it round the first hairpin bend (i.e. ignore the first signposted path which would lead to Blaen y Nant). Not far beyond this turn, a waymarker on the left points to a path that climbs to another forestry track, which it meets at a corner. Turn right here but watch out for a waymark on the left. This path climbs through recently cleared forestry.

The narrow path climbs steadily through the forest, crossing two more forestry roads before arriving at the open hillside beyond a step stile in the perimeter fence. A muddy path through heather and marshy ground now leads to the ridge where you turn left to follow the fence to Creigiau Gleision's northern summit. After descending to a heathery depression, a narrow path climbs to the higher south summit.

Descent
Keep to the east side of the ridge fence. The path down to the forest begins from a marshy depression just beyond a left turn in the ridge fence. The fence shown on the OS Explorer map as accompanying the path no longer exists; just a few rotted fence posts mark its course. Waymarkers make route-finding easy through the forest. Ignore the last waymarker placed on the right of the apex of a forestry road zigzag above Llyn Crafnant; this one will take you to the head of the valley at Blaen-y-nant. Instead stay with the forestry road as it slants downhill and above the shores of Llyn Crafnant.

Creigiau Gleision

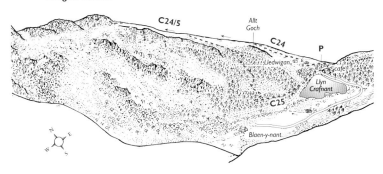

83

Route C26

Capel Curig and Llyn y Coryn

A quick route but better as a descent

Start: Capel Curig car park behind Joe
    Brown's outdoor shop (GR: SH 720582)

Distance: 3 miles/5km

Height gain: 1700ft/520m

Time: 2 hours

After heading back to the road junction in front of the Pinnacle Café, go over a ladder stile between the war memorial and the little church of St Curig and cross a field, aiming left of the Capel Curig Pinnacles (Y Pincin). Over another ladder stile the path crosses a small stream via a slabbed bridge and, now paved with stone slabs, heads east across rough pastureland on the north side of the Pinnacles.

After entering some oak woodland, watch out for a very narrow path climbing left away from the main path. This levels out as it comes to the top of the woods and turns right. Beyond the woods a grass path cuts across a clearing filled with bracken to reach a steep path on the far side. This climbs left to a ladder stile, beyond which it climbs half-right to scale another ladder stile. You are now high on the sides of Clogwyn-mawr, and to the right lies the deep hollow of Nant y Geuallt.

Now follow the fence on the left over level grassland. Beyond another stile the path climbs a steep rock and heather knoll before continuing through an avenue of crag. Go over a ladder stile in a fence that comes in from the right. The path now follows the fence before descending slightly to the east shores of Llyn y Coryn. Beyond the lake the path divides. Take the lower left fork (the upper path is heading for Crimpiau). This skirts the west side of the Crimpiau ridge.

As the ground drops away to the left, the path rounds the head of the hollow of Cwm Llewesig to reach the col between Crimpiau and Craig Wen. On reaching this, the path climbs over the left shoulder of Craig Wen and keeps to the left of the crest until the last moment, when it climbs right to Creigiau Gleision's south summit.

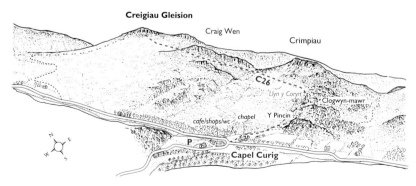

84

Other route options

A path from the A5 north of Capel Curig leads to the bridge at the southern end of Llyn Cowlyd where you can climb north-east up grass then heather slopes to Gleision's southern summit. The 'right to roam' legislation means that those walkers could follow the banks of the Afon Llewesig from the gate at GR 721587 to reach the col between Crimpiau and Craig Wen. Two of the classic routes are by way of Crimpiau from either Capel Curig or Crafnant (see Routes C21/22) and the continuation along the ridge. They're both entertaining from first to last, staying on rock-and-heather ridges for most of the day.

RIDGE ROUTES

Crimpiau

Distance: 1¾ miles/2km
Height gain: 1180ft/360m
Time: 1 hour

Although you can clamber over the rock knolls of the crest, the main path keeps them to the left as it descends from the higher northern summit and over the right shoulder of Craig Wen, beyond which there's a descent to the head of Cwm Llewesig. The narrow path now climbs steeply up to the heather-and-crag summit of Crimpiau.

Below: Craig Wen (left) and Creigiau Gleision (right), seen from above Llyn Coryn on Route C26.

With the odd meaning of the witch's slide, Pen Llithrig y Wrach does have a menacing look when the sun forsakes its slopes. It's the outlying peak both in a roller-coaster east ridge thrown out by Carnedd Llewelyn and a long north-east ridge that declines to Dolgarrog in the Conwy Valley.

Seen from the Capel Curig direction, the mountain is an impressive grassy whaleback, but it's hiding its best features. Get a little bit higher and you'll see the crag-fringed scree slopes that plunge to the western shoreline of Llyn Cowlyd Reservoir, the deepest lake in Wales at 230ft/70m. Walk through Cwm Eigiau to see even more precipitous flanks,

highlighted by a triangle of crags below the summit which stares down on the ruins of the Eigiau slate mines. These would once have reverberated to the sound of gunpowder and the hubbub of several hundred miners.

While the north ridge is heathery with little rocks until the summit dome, most of the mountain's high places are covered with thin grasses, which have eroded to a gravelly surface close to well-used paths.

To the west, Pen Llithrig y Wrach's slopes drop down to the sullen grassy hollow of Cwm Tal-y-braich and the eerie Bwlch Tri-marchog (pass of the three horsemen), which lies over 520ft/160m below the summit and separates Cwm Eigiau from the Llugwy valley and Capel Curig.

Opposite: Pen Llithrig y Wrach from near Capel Curig.
Below: Looking across Bwlch Trimarchog to Pen yr Helgi Du.

Route C27
Cwm Eigiau and the North Ridge

Involves a rough climb near the start
Start: Eigiau car park (GR: SH 783774)
Distance: 3¼ miles/6km
Height gain: 1440ft/440m
Time: 2½ hours

From the car park follow the stony track into the jaws of Cwm Eigiau, rounding the breached dam before turning right to reach the whitewashed cottage of Hafod-y-rhiw. Turn left (trackless at first) up the hill to join what becomes a narrow path through heather. This becomes marshy and overgrown in places but stays to the left of the crags.

On reaching the heathery ridge, watch out for a narrow track on the right. This tackles the crags to the right and continues over a delightful series of rocky knolls, highlighted by views of Eigiau's lakes and the immense cliffs of Craig yr Ysfa. The path descends slightly to a depression preceding Pen Llithrig y Wrach's grassy north ridge. The fence can be crossed 20m left of where the path confronts it (by an intersection of fences at GR 727639).

Continue along the grass and heather ridge, passing a couple of shallow pools. The views of Cwm Eigiau are ever-improving, with Carnedd Llewelyn now standing out from behind Craig yr Ysfa. Eventually the ground steepens and roughens and the path clambers among boulders to reach the summit.

Route C28
Cwm Eigiau and Bwlch Trimarchog

Easy start; very steep to the pass
Start: Eigiau car park (GR: SH 783774)
Distance: 3¼ miles/6km
Height gain: 1380ft/420m
Time: 2–2½ hours

From the car park follow Route C25 past the dam. Just before reaching Hafod-y-rhiw, take the right fork, a bouldery, undulating track which continues high above the Eigiau reservoir and into the inner cwm. Take the right fork again, dropping down towards the dilapidated Cedryn farmhouse before taking the left fork.

The grassy, reed-lined track leads to Cedryn, beyond which a collapsed wall can be followed on an otherwise trackless stretch of rough grassy terrain. Above, on the slopes of Pen Llithrig y Wrach, are the redundant workings of slate quarries. Soon you arrive beneath the steep shadowy slopes of Pen Llithrig y Wrach and Pen yr Helgi Du. The only way is up. The course is tortuously steep and guided to the top by a fence. Breathers may be necessary, if only to look at the improving views back to Llyn Eigiau.

The ladder stile on Bwlch Trimarchog cannot come soon enough. After crossing it, a good path climbs left. It's over grassy terrain at first but this becomes stony on the final approach to Pen Llithrig y Wrach's summit.

Above: On the north ridge of Pen Llithrig y Wrach (Route C27).
Overleaf: Craig Eigiau and the Eigiau Reservoir from the north ridge of Pen Llithrig y Wrach.

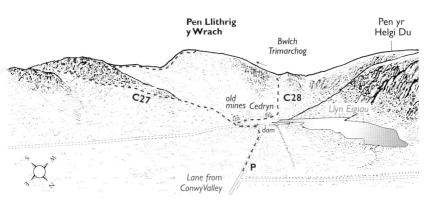

Route C29
Capel Curig and Tal-y-waun

Terrain a bit squelchy in the early stages

Start: Capel Curig car park behind Joe
   Brown's outdoor shop (GR: SH 720582)
Distance: 3 miles/5km
Height gain: 1970ft/600m
Time: 2 hours

From the Pinnacle Café, turn left along the A5 Bangor road. Take care: the footpath is quite narrow and the traffic is fast. After half a mile/800m, take the footpath on the right-hand side of the road, following it uphill and left behind the cottage of Tal-y-waun. Beyond the cottage, the old bridleway passes through gorse scrub but stays close to a drystone wall on the left (rather than the diagonal course shown on current maps). It then veers right by an old wall and fence before crossing at a ladder stile.

The well-defined bridleway now heads north across stark moorland with the angular peak of Pen Llithrig y Wrach in view ahead. Eventually a fence joins in from the right and guides the route to a bridge across a water leat. The path bears left by a wire fence towards the col between the slopes of Pen Llithrig y Wrach and Creigiau Gleision, before crossing another bridge over a stream (GR 717609). Don't be lured on to Llyn Cowlyd's shoreline path but climb the stony slopes to the left winding around rocky outcrops, before continuing north on a steepish grassy spur which leads to Pen Llithrig y Wrach's summit.

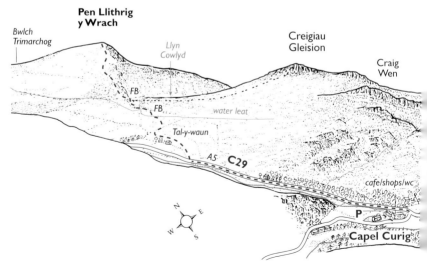

RIDGE ROUTES

Pen yr Helgi Du

Distance: 1¼ miles/2km

Height gain: 660ft/200m

Time: 1 hour

Above: Looking across the northern crags of Pen yr Helgi Du backed up by Carnedd Lewelyn.

From the summit, head north-west across the stony plateau towards the edge overlooking Cwm Eigiau. A good path develops, winding down steep scree then grass slopes to the deep pass of Bwlch Trimarchog. Pen yr Helgi Du's west ridge is grassier but almost as steep. The path stays fairly close to the Cwm Eigiau rim with great views of the mountain's great northern crags and improving views of the tremendous buttresses of Craig yr Ysfa.

From Capel Curig, Pen yr Helgi Du (the hill of the black hound) and its grassy whaleback ridge, Y Braich, looks to be the twin of neighbouring Pen Llithrig y Wrach. However, unlike that peak, Pen yr Helgi Du doesn't have a north ridge: it ends abruptly and spectacularly with cliff-topped flanks which plunge into Cwm Eigiau over 1000ft/300m below.

Perhaps Pen yr Helgi Du's best feature is its view, for across Eigiau are Craig yr Ysfa and its Amphitheatre, and visitors have the best seats in the house to watch climbers grappling with the spectacular cliffs and rock-faces. Craig yr Ysfa reciprocates: the view from the top of the Amphitheatre Buttress reveals Pen yr Helgi Du to be a well-sculpted pyramid with slopes that flow with graceful arcs and runnels to the valley bottom.

The rich colours of the bilberry, heather, scree runs and vegetated crag seem to enhance the slopes more than the hard rock cliffs ever could have done on their own. Also plainly visible from the top of the Amphitheatre is the deep pass of Bwlch Eryl Farchog, and the little path that tackles the spiky rocks of Pen yr Helgi Du's north-west spur. This short pull is the easiest but most exhilarating of scrambles – the sort you don't want to end.

Pen yr Helgi Du looks and is a very fine place to be.

Opposite: Craig yr Ysfa and Carnedd Llewelyn.
Below: Pen yr Helgi Du from Bwlch Eryl Farchog.

Route C30

Cwm Eigiau and Bwlch Eryl Farchog

Involves a steep climb from out of the cwm

Start: Eigiau car park (GR: SH783774)

Distance: 4¼ miles/7km

Height gain: 1570ft/480m

Time: 2½ hours

From the car park follow the track up the valley and round the breached dam. Just before reaching the whitewashed cottage of Hafod-y-rhiw take the right fork, a bouldery, undulating track which continues high above the Eigiau reservoir and into the inner cwm. Take the right fork again, dropping down towards the dilapidated Cedryn farmhouse before turning right on the track that crosses the Afon Eigiau.

After passing a climbers' hut, the track ends at the slate mine barracks near to the head of the cwm. Go through the barracks and re-cross the stream on a dam/causeway, then turn right beneath the piles of slate on a narrow path that fizzles out on a bouldery raised island surrounded by marshy moorland. Beyond it a narrow path heads towards the huge cliffs of Craig yr Ysfa. The path now aims for the incredibly steep slopes to the left of the cliffs.

Several small paths peel off right to the various climbing grounds but keep to the narrow path that zigzags through heather and bilberry and flirts with a bouldery gully before, in the upper stages, veering left to reach the pass of Bwlch Eryl Farchog.

From here you join the popular Carnedd Llewelyn route from the Ogwen Valley, but for this route you turn in the opposite direction (left) to climb Pen yr Helgi Du. The path is an entertaining one, scrambling up steep rocky slopes. You'll need to use your hands occasionally but in good conditions there's nothing serious. Suddenly the rocks end and the path deposits you on an easy grass ridge with just a short stroll to the summit cairn.

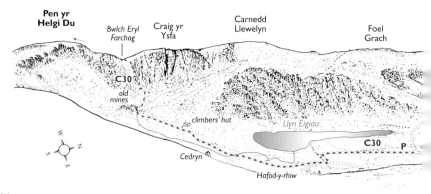

Route C31
Gwern Gof Isaf and Y Braich
Pleasant route, especially in descent, along a smooth, grassy ridge

Start: Gwern Gof Isaf camp site car park near Capel Curig (pay at farm) (GR: SH 686602)

Distance: 4¼ miles/7km

Height gain: 1480ft/450m

Time: 2½ hours

From Gwern Gof Isaf farm, follow the A5 for a quarter of a mile/400m back towards Capel Curig. Ignoring the tarmac reservoir road, take the next signed track on the left heading for Tal y Braich farm. Look for the faint path on the left before the farm (marked in dashes on the Outdoor Leisure map) and follow it across rough sheep pasture.

This climbs to a water leat at the base of Y Braich, which is Pen yr Helgi Du's south ridge. After crossing a bridge over the leat and a ladder stile just beyond, climb the grassy rock-interspersed whaleback ridge, which offers glimpses into the hollow of Cwm Tal-y-braich and the craggier Cwm Llugwy. For much of the way the small reservoir of Ffynnon Llugwy stays out of sight, unless you divert to the western rim.

After about 1½ miles/2.5km you arrive on the grassy dome which is Pen yr Helgi Du. After the gentle and affable nature of this route, it will come as quite a surprise to look over the fierce northern crags that overlook Cwm Eigiau.

RIDGE ROUTES

Pen Llithrig y Wrach
Distance: 1¼ miles/2km

Height gain: 510ft/155m

Time: 1 hour

Descend steep grass slopes on a clear path which hugs the Cwm Eigiau rim as it des-

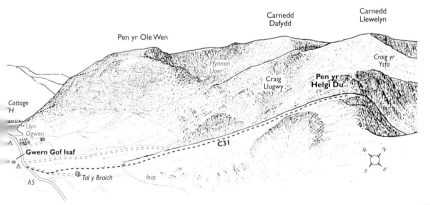

cends to Bwlch Trimarchog. A steep slog, on grass at first but on rock and scree slopes higher up, now begins up Pen Llithrig y Wrach's west spur. The summit lies to the south-east.

Carnedd Llewelyn

Distance: 1½ miles/2.5km
Height gain: 1020ft/310m
Time: 1 hour

A very steep, narrow path clambers down the rocky west spur of Pen yr Helgi Du – you'll need to use your hands in places, but in normal conditions it's not difficult and the tremendous views of Caig yr Ysfa and its Amphitheatre Buttress more than compensate for any difficulty. At the pass of Bwlch Eryl Farchog the main Ogwen path is joined. Now climb to the top of Craig yr Ysfa. There's one easy rock scramble (NB this could be very tricky in snow or ice conditions). From here you can look down the Amphitheatre and see the climbers on the crag faces. The path continues north-west up the stony slopes of Penywaun-wen, a bouldery finale which takes the route to the summit wind shelters.

Below: Pen yr Helgi Du at the head of Cwm Eigiau.

CARNEDD LLEWELYN

The third-highest mountain in Wales is named after Llewelyn the Great, the 13th-century Prince of Wales who held court from his castle at nearby Abergwyngregyn. A great hulk of a mountain, it is set right in the centre of the range, some 2½ miles/4km from the nearest road. As such it's often invisible from the valley floors – the walker often has to climb to see it.

Carnedd Llewelyn has no distinctive shape nor elegance of form. It's a huge, domed colossus made from hard volcanic dolerite. The vastness of its stony summit and the numerous cairns and wind shelters mean that the mountain is hard to navigate when the cloud hangs low. As the mountain sends out four lofty ridges covering all corners of the compass, it would be easy in such conditions to find yourself on the wrong one. Always take a compass or GPS with you on the Carneddau. Of the ridges, the short rocky

Below: Craig yr Ysfa's Amphitheatre.

arête linking the mountain with Yr Elen is the finest, while the 6-mile/10km ridge to Bwlch y Dduefaen, taking in three more 3000ft peaks, is the longest.

Although I've said it has no distinctive shape, Carnedd Llewelyn does possess some spectacular sights, none more so than Craig yr Ysfa at the head of Cwm Eigiau. Huge buttresses, well-loved by climbers, surround the vast Amphitheatre and its dark scree gully.

Llewelyn has two tiny tarns: the tiny Ffynnon Llyffant (the frog's well) huddles in a bouldery eastern cwm, while Ffynnon Caseg (the mare's well) occupies the deep cwm between Llewelyn and Yr Elen. Both are magical destinations in their own right.

Route C32
Cefn Tal-llyn Eigiau

A stimulating wilderness route

Start: Eigiau car park (GR: SH 783774)
Distance: 4¼ miles/7km
Height gain: 2300ft/700m
Time: 2½ hours

Follow the stony track which heads WNW towards the rocks of Clogwynyreryr. Where the track divides, take the higher left fork, which soon swings right beneath rock and heather slopes before arcing left into the cwm of Afon Dulyn. At the second ladder stile in Cwm Dulyn (GR 718667) leave the track for a faint path raking up to the ridge wall on Cefn Tal-llyn-Eigiau.

The path stays by the wall/fence until it reaches the northernmost rocks of Craig Eigiau, then traverses a vast moorland plateau

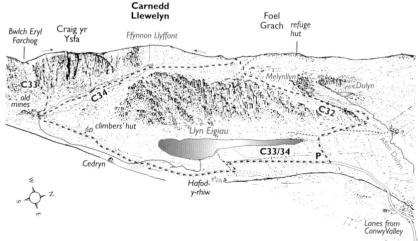

to the north-west of the rocks. Notable in the views to the right are the cliff-ringed twin lakes of Melynllyn and Dulyn, set high on the slopes of Foel Grach and Foel-fras respectively. The path passes to the right of a shallow pool, traverses an area flanked to the east by peat hags, then begins the climb over grassy moorland towards a prominent rock outcrop to the right of Carnedd Llewelyn. The path fades high on the ridge but by maintaining direction you'll reach the main ridge path by the outcrop. Now turn left along the ridge path, with the tiny tarn of Ffynnon Llyffant in its stony cwm appearing on the left just before the final climb to Llewelyn's bouldery summit.

Descent

This path is especially fine in descent, perhaps the best in the whole of the Carneddau. The secret is to find its beginning. Once you pass the prominent rock castle above Ffynnon Llyffant, look below left and you should see a path arcing around Foel Grach's southeast slopes towards the moorland marked on the map as Gledrffordd. The way is remarkably easy-paced and you can stride out across grassland towards the distant rock crest of Craig Eigiau. The main path just skirts the rocks though there's an easy detour to the summit if you have enough time. After following the ridge fence and wall along Cefn Tal-y-llyn Eigiau, the path descends to a ladder stile on the Melynllyn reservoir track. Turn right along this to head back to the Cwm Eigiau car parks, ignoring all side tracks.

Route C33
Cwm Eigiau and Bwlch Eryl Farchog
An adventurous route where the walker
*   mingles with the climber*
Start: Eigiau car park (GR: SH 783774)
Distance: 4¾ miles/7.5km
Height gain: 2400ft/730m
Time: 2½ –3 hours

From the car park at the end of the lane, head south along the stony reservoir road which leads on directly to the Eigiau dam, where it turns left across the bridge over the outflow. At the far end turn right before taking the lower right fork to pass beneath the white-washed cottage of Hafod-y-rhiw and the immense crags of Craig Eigiau, which soar from the far side of the shallow lake.

The bouldery, undulating track skirts the stony lower slopes of Pen Llithrig y Wrach's northern ridge. Just before reaching the decaying cottage of Cedryn, descend to the valley bottom on a right fork track which soon crosses the Afon Eigiau. The track then climbs past a climbers' hut before terminating by some ruined quarry workings and barracks. Now close to the head of Cwm Eigiau, the situation is completely dominated by Craig yr Ysfa and its Amphitheatre, a huge scree-filled gully flanked by frightening cliffs and buttresses.

Overleaf: The summit of Craig Eigiau.

101

Beyond the barracks the route re-crosses the stream on a dam/causeway. It now turns right beneath the piles of slate on a narrow path which fades for a short distance as you continue along a bouldery mound surrounded by marshy moorland. Beyond it a narrow path heads towards the huge cliffs of Craig yr Ysfa before winding up incredibly steep slopes to the left of the cliffs. Several small paths peel off right to the various climbing grounds but keep to the narrow path which zigzags through heather and bilberry, and flirts with a bouldery gully before, in the upper stages, veering left to reach the pass of Bwlch Eryl Farchog.

Turn right here along a narrowing ridge then scramble up a short section of rock slabs above Craig yr Ysfa. From here you can look down the Amphitheatre and along the length of Cwm Eigiau.

Now the path climbs north-west up the stony slopes of Penywaun-wen before making a final assault on Carnedd Llewelyn's east ridge. Near the top you can look down right into a bouldery cwm where a tiny lake, Ffynnon Llyffant, basks in the total isolation of its stony cwm. A bouldery finale leads to the summit wind shelters.

Opposite: Ffynnon Llyffant, Carnedd Llewelyn.

Route C34
Cwm Eigiau and Ffynnon Llyffant

A seldom-used way which is trackless in the upper reaches

Start: Eigiau car park (GR: SH 783774)
Distance: 5 miles/8km
Height gain: 2400ft/730m
Time: 3 hours

As in Route C30, walk up the stony track past the reservoir, turn right beyond the dam, take the right fork by the cottage of Hafod-y-rhiw and the next right fork to cross the stream and pass the climbers' hut to reach the ruined mine buildings. Now follow the banks of the Afon Eigiau to the right side of the cliffs and gullies of Craig yr Ysfa and continue with it northwards up the hillside (note: this is not the right of way marked on the OS map).

The stream divides, and you follow the tributary that stays close to the crags and outcrops on the left. It will lead you across rough pathless slopes to Ffynnon Llyffant (the frog's well), a romantic shallow tarn huddled in a bouldery hollow beneath Carnedd Llewelyn.

To avoid the direct assault up the craggy slopes above the tarn (feasible for the experienced walker), climb the grassy slopes on the right, heading towards the saddle of Gwaun y Garnedd. Here you'll be able to pick up the Cefn Tal-y-llyn Eigiau path used on Route C31 and follow it to the left, past the rock castle on the main ridge. Beyond this there's an easy path over stony ground to reach Llewelyn's summit.

Route C35

Ffynnon Llugwy and Craig yr Ysfa

*A dull start but things get spectacular once
    the ridge is gained*

Start: Gwern Gof Isaf farm car parking (toll)
    (GR: SH 685604)

Distance: 3½ miles/5.5km

Height gain: 2530ft/770m

Time: 2½ hours

Turn right along the road towards Capel Curig
then leave it for a tarred water company road
on the left. This climbs steeply up the hillsides
and beneath the west flanks of Pen yr Helgi
Du. Where the road swings left towards Ffynnon Llugwy Reservoir, leave it for a right fork
ahead that continues along the lake's east
shores before raking up scaly slopes to Bwlch
y Eryl Farchog, a splendid grassy pass between Carnedd Llewelyn and Pen yr Helgi
Du. Here you have superb views across the
head of Cwm Eigiau to Craig yr Ysfa and its
Amphitheatre.

Turn left here along a narrowing ridge
where the upper slopes are cloaked in
heather and bilberry. Soon you're faced with
a short scramble on rock slabs topping Craig
yr Ysfa. From here you can look down the
length of Cwm Eigiau to see Pen yr Helgi Du
and Pen Llithrig y Wrach, twin grassy whaleback ridges which end abruptly in impressive, ice-carved northern crags.

Now the path climbs north-west up the
stony slopes of Penywaun-wen before making a final assault on Carnedd Llewelyn's east
ridge. Near the top you can look down right
into a bouldery cwm filled by a tiny lake,
Ffynnon Llyffant.

*Opposite: Carnedd Llewelyn and Penywaun-
wen reflecting in the still waters of Ffynnon
Llugwy Reservoir at twilight.*

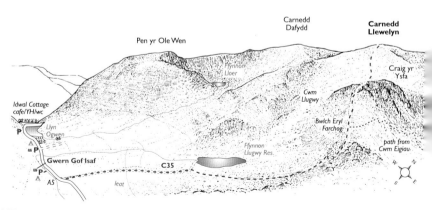

Route C36
Cwm Caseg and Cwm Bychan

A sullen route with a spectacular finale
Start: Bethesda car park (GR: SH 622668)
Distance: 5 miles/8km
Height gain: 3020ft/920m
Time: 3 hours

Although walkers could probably find a parking place somewhere on the streets of Gerlan, their cars often cause inconvenience to locals, so again I've started the route from the riverside car park in Bethesda's town centre. From here head back to the High Street and turn right. Turn left on the street signed to Pen y Bryn School before taking the right fork, Pant Glas Road, which is signed 'to Gerlan'. At the next crossroads go straight ahead along Ffordd Gerlan, which is Gerlan's main street. Turn left along the lane at the end of the houses and follow it up the hillside past several cottages. The lane degenerates into a cart track, which terminates at a gate (GR 639665) at the south-western foot of Gyrn Wigau.

Beyond the gate turn right along a grassy, sometimes muddy track heading east along the top edge of some fields and parallel to the

Afon Caseg. Stay with the main track until it ends at the tall, walled enclosures by the ancient settlements. Intermittent paths take the route around the cwm high above the river, as the hill slopes of Yr Elen and Garnedd Uchaf close in, hiding the inner cwm beyond. Cross the Afon Wen to the left of the large complex of sheepfolds. Beyond the crossing a prominent track skirts the bouldery slopes of Clogwyn Yr Heliwr. The track becomes a faint path as it traverses the mosses of the inner cwm to reach the crags of Carreg-y-Gath at the foot of Cwm Bychan (GR 678656). Here a stream tumbles down some crags to form an attractive waterfall.

Now the real climb begins. Ford the stream around 50m below the waterfall and climb the spur, keeping clear of the crags on the right. The view into the upper corrie of Cwm Caseg, with its lake surrounded by the screes and crags of Yr Elen and Carnedd Llewelyn, will leave you spellbound and help to keep your mind off the toil of this steep spur.

This pathless course leads to the saddle of Gwaun y Garnedd, where you join the main Carneddau ridge path. Turn right along it as it eases over grassy, then bouldery terrain to Carnedd Llewelyn's summit.

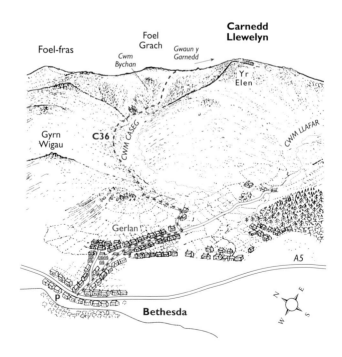

RIDGE ROUTES

Pen Llithrig y Wrach
Distance: 1½ miles/2.5km
Height gain: 230ft/70m
Time: 1 hour

From the summit shelters head ESE along the ridge to the cliffs of Craig yr Ysfa, where there's a dramatic view down a huge gorge known as the Amphitheatre, flanked on the right by the pinnacled ridge of Amphitheatre Buttress. The path comes to a crag with some tricky rock steps – extra care must be exercised in wet or icy conditions. Below the crag it continues to Bwlch Eryl Farchog, the col between Craig yr Ysfa and Pen yr Helgi Du. Beyond this there's an entertaining but short ascent to Pen yr Helgi Du by a steep path that threads between crags interspersed with bilberry and heather, where a steadying hand is occasionally needed.

Yr Elen
Distance: 1 mile/1.5km
Height gain: 160ft/50m
Time: ¾ hour

This is the most splendid ridge in the Carneddau. Unfortunately it's over all too soon. Yr Elen is invisible from Carnedd Llewelyn's summit, so the walker has to go to the western rim. Don't stray too far north or there will be more boulders to cross on the initial descent. A good path does develop and descends the rocky rim at the head of Cwm Caseg. The little lake of Ffynnon Caseg comes into view. On reaching the col, the path up Yr Elen eases away from the edge, although a good option in good conditions is to clamber over the rocky arête all the way to the top – or stay as close to it as possible and round the crags you don't fancy tackling.

Foel Grach
Distance: 1 mile/1.5km
Height gain: 130ft/40m
Time: ½ hour

Head north on the main Carneddau highway, down rocks at first but then grass. These days there's a well-defined path all the way. In mist make sure you don't drift right and get on to the much fainter path over Gledffordd.

Below: Rugged Yr Elen and its lake, Ffynnon Caseg, seen from Garnedd Uchaf.

Although it's a 3000-footer, the slender, angular peak of Yr Elen is little more than the sidekick of Carnedd Llewelyn, whose massive girth and height dwarf its smaller outlier. Yr Elen, the hill of the fawn, lies hidden from view from many angles, but seen from Bethesda and the north-west valleys of the Caseg and Llafar, it comes into its own, dominating the mountainscape. From here, even Llewelyn becomes the backstage scenery.

The main problem with Yr Elen is that the valleys of the Caseg and Llafar, while they are wild and enticing, are very wet underfoot, and their rivers are not easily forded. Steep slopes of horrid loose scree cover three sides of the mountain's upper slopes. Walkers often arrive on the summit with wet feet and soggy mud-stained socks. There is an answer, but it involves Carnedd Llewelyn again. Climb to Llewelyn first then descend west. Here you'll see Yr Elen's best feature: a splendid rocky arête that climbs from the col to its summit – it's short but provides spectacular views. On one side the Black Ladders cliffs glare across Cwm Llafar, and on the other side there's a sparkling, tiny tarn, Ffynnon Caseg, huddled in its stony cwm.

Opposite: Yr Elen seen from the rapidly narrowing valley of the Afon Caseg.

Route C37
Bethesda Cwm Caseg and Ffynnon Caseg
A strenuous route with a little scrambling at the end
Start: Bethesda car park (GR: SH 622668)
Distance: 5 miles/8km
Height gain: 2790ft/850m
Time: 3 hours

From the riverside car park in Bethesda return to the High Street and turn right along it before turning left on a street signed to Pen y Bryn School. Take the right fork, Pant Glas Road, which is signed 'to Gerlan'. At the next crossroads go straight ahead along Ffordd Gerlan, which is Gerlan's main street. Turn left along the lane at the end of the houses on the left and follow it up the hillside. The lane degenerates into a cart track terminating at a gate by some sheep pens (GR 639665).

A grassy track now leads right, delving into Cwm Caseg and keeping high above but parallel to the river. Stay with the main track until it ends at the tall walled enclosures marked as settlements on the map. An intermittent path now continues high on the left side of the cwm – this is a much drier course than the right of way shown on the map. It meets the course of an old water leat, now grassed over and rush-filled. The leat leads the route to the Afon Wen, which should be forded just to the left of a complex of sheepfolds.

A prominent track now skirts the boulders and crags of Clogwyn yr Heliwr, then fades

111

into the mosses of the upper cwm. From here a narrow path reaches the foot of Cwm Bychan, where a stream tumbles down some crags to form an attractive waterfall. Looking up to the sky above it you'll see the craggy, domed summit of Garnedd Uchaf.

Beyond the stream, you cross intermittent paths and climb above the mossy springs that feed the main Caseg stream. Cross the Caseg below a grassy knoll before climbing left of the knoll to enter the upper cwm. You'll be looking down on Ffynnon Caseg, a secretive tarn surrounded by the crag and screes of Carnedd Llewelyn (left) and Yr Elen (right). This is a wonderful spot for lunch and maybe a rest before the pull to the summit.

Now comes the hard part. It's a steady climb north-westwards up grass and stone slopes to the ridge. The crest is a mixture of rock and scree. Sometimes you need to keep left of the crags, at others you need to be on the crest itself. It's a sporty little clamber but it takes very little time.

Route C38
Bethesda and Cwm Caseg
A strenuous, wild and barren route
Start: Bethesda car park (GR: SH 622668)
Distance: 4 miles/6.5km
Height gain: 2850ft/870m
Time: 2½ hours

Note: The Caseg can be difficult to ford and this route is only recommended for dry periods or in the summer months

---

Follow Route C37 from the riverside car park in Bethesda to Gerlan and turn left along the lane at the end of the houses to the gate at GR 639665. Follow a grassy track on the right into Cwm Caseg, keeping high above but parallel to the river. Across the sombre moors of the cwm, the crags of Carnedd Dafydd and Yr Elen's summit cone dominate the scene.

Often, outside the summer months, the track can be waterlogged and walkers usually climb on to the grassy banks to the left. Just past a quarry take the less obvious grassy right fork, then turn right along a narrow path heading south-west to ford the Afon Caseg.

Cross the stream carefully and continue up tussocky slopes to Yr Elen's west ridge. A steady plod begins on grass at first and then on a little rock at Foel Ganol. The final 500ft over steep and loose shaly slopes is unpleasant, especially in descent.

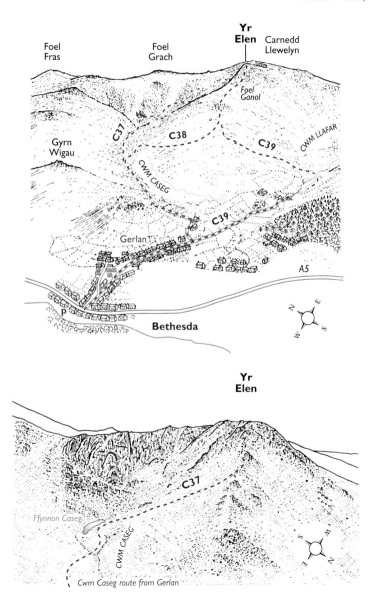

Foel
Fras

Foel
Grach

**Yr
Elen**

Carnedd
Llewelyn

*Foel
Ganol*

C37

C38

C39

CWM LLAFAR

Gyrn
Wigau

CWM CASEG

C39

Gerlan

A5

P

Bethesda

**Yr
Elen**

C37

Ffynnon Caseg

CWM CASEG

Cwm Caseg route from Gerlan

113

Route C39
Bethesda and Cwm Lafar

A strenuous route but a rather dull climb on the other side of Yr Elen

Start: Bethesda car park (GR: SH 622668)
Distance: 3¼ miles/6km
Height gain: 2850ft/870m
Time: 2½ hours

Follow Route C37 out of the town and uphill to Gerlan village, but this time go straight ahead past all the houses. In its last few yards the lane swings right to cross the Afon Lafar just below the farming complex of Gwaun-y-gwiail.

Turn left along a short drive marked private, before climbing the ladder stile into a field. The path now skirts the left edge of the field, passing close to the old water works which is on the other side of a slate fence. Several waymarking posts direct the route left then right into another field and around the ruins of an old farmstead. After crossing a stream (Afon Cenllusg) on a stone slab bridge, the route climbs towards the larger Afon Llafar, whose course leads over rushy terrain to a ladder stile at the edge of the access area.

The clear path stays parallel to the south banks of the Llafar, passing an enclosure bound by iron railings and a derelict dam. By this time Yr Elen rears up quite impressively into the sky, beckoning you across the dank intervening moors and the Llafar. Find a safe crossing then head across the wet, tussocky moorland terrain to gain Yr Elen's west ridge, where you follow Route C38 over grass then scree to the summit.

RIDGE ROUTE

Carnedd Llewelyn

Distance: 1 mile/1.5km
Height gain: 460ft/140m
Time: ¼ hour

After descending the splendid arête overlooking Cwm Caseg, the route tackles the boulder-strewn slopes of Carnedd Llewelyn. In the later stages easier, less bouldery, terrain can be found on the right.

Opposite: Yr Elen's glorious south-east arête, seen from the slopes of Carnedd Llewellyn. This is one of the most enjoyable paths in the Central Carneddau.

Like Yr Elen, Foel Grach (scabby bare hill) is a bit overshadowed by Carnedd Llewelyn. Were it not for the convenient stone refuge hut built into its summit boulders, the mountain would persuade few to dally on their way to the Carneddau's highest peak. However, Foel Grach is like an uncut, unpolished precious stone, lacking distinctive form but with understated majesty. It's an angular, grassy peak fringed with crags and boulders which overlook the long cwms of Caseg and Dulyn.

At the head of the latter are two of the most dramatic but least-visited tarns in Snowdonia – Dulyn (black lake) and Melynllyn (yellow lake). Both are cradled by cliffs, but are set so deeply in their hollows that you have to get right up to them for a view. Dulyn, as its name suggests, has waters that are dark and mysteriously deep, its banks plunging to over 50ft/15m deep less than 1m from the shoreline. It has been said that some time in the past Melynllyn had a stone pier, and if anybody came here at Halloween they would witness the ghosts of those who were about to die walking along it before disappearing into the waters.

Foel Grach's high eastern slopes above the lakes are marshy and hard going. On the west side the mountain throws out a little spur, Clogwyn yr Heliwr, which encloses the stony Cwm Wen and declines into the valley of the Caseg. To the south of this spur is Cwm Bychan, a tight ravine of stones and crag dividing Foel Grach from the gargantuan slopes of Carnedd Llewelyn.

Opposite: Looking across Clogwyn Heliwr to Garnedd Uchaf and Foel-fras. Right: Approaching the crossing of the Afon Wen, with Yr Elen on the right and the jaws of Cwm Caseg directly ahead.

Route C40
Cwm Dulyn and its lakes

A seldom-used route visiting two secretive
crag-ringed tarns

Start: Eigiau car park (GR: SH 731633)
Distance: 3 miles/5km
Height gain: 2065ft/630m
Time: 2 hours

Follow the stony track which heads WNW towards the rocks of Clogwynyreryr. Where the track divides, take the higher left fork, which soon swings right beneath rock and heather slopes before arcing left into the cwm of Afon Dulyn. The rolling northern Carneddau 3000ers of Foel Grach, Garnedd Uchaf and Foel-fras punctuate the horizon. While the crags that surround Dulyn's high cwm come into view at this stage, the waters of its small reservoir are hidden behind a grassy

spur. After passing beneath the ruined buildings and shattered rocks of the Melynllyn Hone Quarry, the track turns left to reach the stony northern shore of Melynllyn.

Go across the plank bridge which spans the outflow, but ignore the prominent path to the right (this descends to the Dulyn Reservoir). Instead take the faint path climbing up the spur between the two lakes. The Dulyn Reservoir now appears below Foel-fras. It's a much grander scene than its neighbour, surrounded by crags and almost completely enclosed by the arms of the mountain; just one nick allows the water to flow into the river below.

Halfway up the spur, the faint paths divide, and you take the right fork. Foel Grach has disappeared beyond the concave slopes, but you'll be able to pick out a green swath across the upper slopes to identify the route.

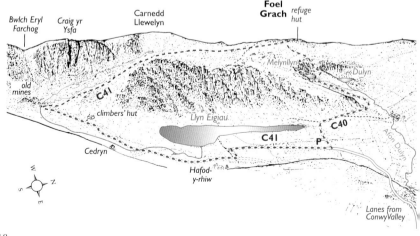

It's a good steady climb and the marshy terrain of the high slopes makes it a bit of a grind in places, but soon the rocky top of Foel Grach reappears, now quite close. Eventually you're joined by a track from the left. Now the going is easy, all the way to the top.

Below: Foel Grach seen from the Cwm Dulyn approach (Route C40).

Route C41
Cwm Eigiau

A seldom-used route with a tough climb out of Cwm Eigiau – good in descent

Start: Eigiau car park (GR: SH 731633)
Distance: 4⅓ miles/7km
Height gain: 2000ft/610m
Time: 2½–3 hours

From the car park at the end of the lane, head south along the stony reservoir road that leads to the Eigiau Dam, where it turns left across the bridge over the outflow. At the far end turn right before taking a right fork track to pass beneath Hafod-y-rhiw, a charming

white-walled dwelling dwarfed by the immense crags of Eigiau, which rise at the far side of the lake. Take the more prominent right fork track on the approach to the ruined cottage of Cedryn.

This crosses the river on a footbridge and enters Cwm Eigiau. Ahead you'll see the peaks of Pen yr Helgi Du and Pen Llithrig-y-wrach, separated by the pass of Bwlch Tri-marchog.

The track ends by some ruined quarry workings and barracks. Here you get a spectacular look at Craig yr Ysfa, which soars to the skies from the head of the cwm. It consists of a huge gorge known as the Amphitheatre and its wide scree fan, flanked on the right by sheer cliffs and on the left by the pinnacled ridge of the Amphitheatre Buttress.

The path bears right uphill to join the east bank of Nant Fawnog, which you follow northwards along a faint path. Where the stream ends, maintain the same direction and you'll come across a wide grass track topping the broad marshy ridge of Gledrffordd. Turn left along this (right for an escape route back to Eigiau) to climb to Foel Grach's summit, whose rocks appear on the north-west skyline in the later stages.

Route C42
Cwm Caseg and Clogwyn yr Heliwr

A fine wilderness route with a steep seldom-trod spur at the end

Start: Bethesda's riverside car park (GR: SH 622668)
Distance: 4¼ miles/7km
Height gain: 2790ft/850m
Time: 2½ hours

From the riverside car park in Bethesda head back to the High Street before turning right. Turn left on the street signed to Pen y Bryn School before taking the right fork, Pant Glas Road, which is signed 'to Gerlan'. At the next crossroads go straight ahead along Ffordd Gerlan, which is Gerlan's main street. Turn left along the lane at the end of the houses and follow it up the hillside past several cottages. The lane degenerates into a cart track, which terminates at a gate (GR 639665).

A grassy track now heads into Cwm Caseg, staying high above but parallel to the river. In good weather you will enjoy excellent views across intervening moorland into Cwm Lafar, dominated by Carnedd Dafydd's great walls of rock.

The track becomes marshy and infested with rushes for a while and walkers have taken to the pastureland on the left. Stay with the main track, ignoring right fork paths just beyond a quarry and on the approach to the settlements, above which there are tall stone-walled enclosures. The track terminates at the settlements and some sheep-walks/paths head towards the river, but by staying on higher ground you'll keep your feet much drier. Intermittent paths do exist at these higher levels and curve around beneath Bera Bach's rocky tor towards the craggy entrance to the Afon Caseg's upper cwm.

The route now comes across a rushy channel, formerly a water-carrying leat, shortly before coming to a large complex of sheepfolds. The Afon Wen should be crossed to the left of these. On the other side a clear track skirts the lower slopes of Clogwyn yr Heliwr, the bouldery spur between Cwm Wen and Cwm Bychan. However, this route forsakes it for a bold route (there is an extremely faint path) straight up the lower grassy slopes of the spur.

This soon leads to some faint zigzags (more visible from above and below than when you're on them), which make the going easier. Above a rash of boulders, keep to the crest of the spur which, from the middle stages, gives a fine view of Ffynnon Caseg, the tarn occupying the craggy hollow between Yr Elen and Carnedd Llewelyn.

The ground steepens in the final stages. Keep left of the high crag guarding the rim of the ridge and aim for the boulders and outcrops that top Foel Grach's summit. The shelter is on the far side of the rocks.

Route C43
Bethesda and the Western Ridge

A splendid striding ridge walk

Start: Bethesda's riverside car park
  (GR: SH 622668)
Distance: 4¾ miles/7.5km
Height gain: 3120ft/950m (over all the tops)
Time: 2½–3 hours

Follow Route C42 from Bethesda's riverside car park to Gerlan and again take the left fork road beyond the houses and stay with it after it degenerates into a rough cart track. Turn right along the grassy track beyond the gate at

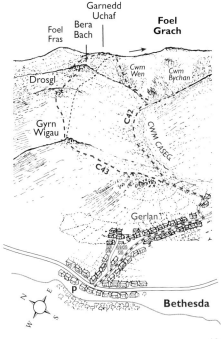

GR 639665, but leave the track at the first slight right-hand bend, where you head north-eastwards across grass and bracken-clad slopes, aiming for a ladder stile on the skyline. Once on the ridge there is a steady climb to the first summit, Gyrn Wigau, whose rocks give a foretaste of things to come.

The bracken and bilberry of the lower ridge give way to grass on the approach to Drosgl. The path divides just short of its summit; the upper one stays on the ridge, while the lower one rakes across the south sides.

Either one will do, but as the day is a long one, maybe the lower is best. The views become ever more spectacular. When the path arrives at the col between Garnedd Uchaf and Foel Grach, you can look directly into the rocky amphitheatre of Cwm Caseg where the little tarn, Ffynnon Caseg, is dwarfed by the crags of Carnedd Llewelyn and the scree slopes of Yr Elen.

The path now climbs directly up Foel Grach's broad grassy north ridge to the bouldery summit, passing the refuge hut en route.

RIDGE ROUTES

Carnedd Llewelyn

Distance: 1 mile/1.5km
Height gain: 430ft/130m
Time: ¼ hour

A clear path heads south, staying close to the west side of the ridge at first, then going straight up an increasingly stony ridge and passing to the left of a castle-like crag before attaining the bouldery summit plateau.

Garnedd Uchaf (Carnedd Gwenllian)

Distance: 2–3 miles/1km
Height gain: 150ft/45m
Time: 1 hour

From the summit head north past the refuge hut before descending a wide path over grassy slopes. Ignore the faint path on the right as this heads directly to Foel-fras, missing out Garnedd Uchaf. Clamber over the rocky mound to the summit.

Craig Eigiau

Distance: 2¼ miles/3.5km
Height gain: 65ft/20m
Time: 1 hour

Ignore the main ridge path heading south towards Carnedd Llewelyn and instead trend left to locate a faint and intermittent path heading SSW around the cwm of Melynllyn. As it eases around the grassy rim of the cwm, the path joins a better-defined one that has come from Carnedd Llewelyn. This heads north-east (to the left) across a flat plateau with distant views of Craig Eigiau's top crags. A narrow path breaks away right on the approach to a rounded grassy knoll (738m spot height) and takes the route by a little lake to the crags. Choose your own summit: there are plenty vying for top spot.

Opposite: Foel Grach from Carnedd Llewelyn.

Carnedd Dafydd, named after the son of Llewelyn the Great, 13th-century Prince of Wales, is the second-highest of the Carnedd range and fourth-highest in all Wales. Dafydd's peak is less of a lump than Llewelyn's, especially when seen across Cwm Lafar, where its craggy north-west ridge rises steadily to reach a nice pointed summit.

Opposite and below: Black Ladders.

Respectfully, Carnedd Dafydd has three ridges, one fewer than Carnedd Llewelyn, but what fine ridges they are! Two, the ones linking Pen yr Ole Wen and Carnedd Llewelyn, never drop below 3000ft and represent the most spectacular and easy-paced walking in the Carneddau. The fascinating north-west ridge, known as Mynydd Du (the black mountain) is enhanced by the remote corries of Cwm Glas Mawr and Cwm Glas Bach and by the spiky Lech Ddu spur. The fierce vegetated cliffs at the head of Cwm Lafar are known as the Black Ladders (Ysgolion Duon), which in days gone by had some of the most popular climbs in Snowdonia.

Route C44
Bethesda and Cwm Lafar

A long but stimulating route
Start: Bethesda's riverside car park
   (GR: SH 622668)
Distance: 3¼ miles/6km
Height gain: 3020ft/920m
Time: 2½ hours

From the car park head back to the High Street and turn right. Turn left on the road signed to Pen y Bryn School then take the right fork, Pant Glas Road, which is signed 'to Gerlan'. At the next crossroads go straight ahead along Ffordd Gerlan, which leads through Gerlan's main street and back out into high country.

Go over the Llafar Bridge at the end of the road before turning left up a short drive marked private, before climbing the ladder stile into a field. The path now skirts the left edge of the field, passing close to the old water works, which is on the other side of a slate fence. Several waymarking posts direct the route left then right into another field before circumventing the ruins of an old farmstead.

After crossing a stream (Afon Cenllusg) on a stone slab bridge, the route climbs towards the larger Afon Llafar, and follows a course over rushy terrain parallel to its south bank. So far the scenes have been of rather sad, neglected countryside but the slopes of Yr Elen and Carnedd Dafydd close in to add drama to the scene. Leave the path near a small enclosure bound by iron railings and climb the pathless, grassy Mynydd Du ridge on the right.

Soon the route looks down into the wild, rocky Cwm Glas Bach, where the Lech Du spur plummets into the main valley. Now, across stony ground with views down Cwm Glas Mawr, the route takes you steadily on steepening ground that offers spectacular views of the Black Ladders, which lie at the head of Cwm Llafar. Soon the gradients ease again on the approach to the cairns on Carnedd Dafydd.

Below: Carnedd Dafydd's north-west ridge.

Above: Carnedd Dafydd from Pen Yr Ole Wen.

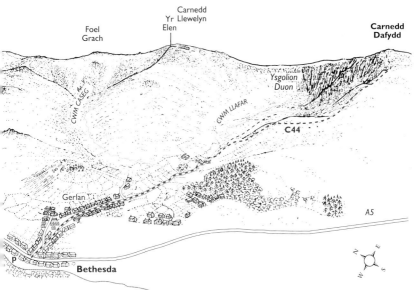

127

Route C45

Ogwen Valley and Craig Llugwy

A climb to a seldom-trodden ridge

Start: Gwern Gof Isaf farm car parking (toll)
  (GR: SH 685604)

Distance: 3 miles/5km

Height gain: 2560ft/780m

Time: 2 hours

Head northwards up a tarred water company road, which is staggered to the right of the camp site, to climb beneath the west flanks of Pen yr Helgi Du. Stay with the road all the way to the shores of Ffynnon Llugwy Reservoir.

Go over the bridge spanning the outflow of the lake, then trace the drystone wall on the left as it climbs well to the left of the precipi-tous cliffs of Craig y Llyn. The wall leads safely to a small pool on the rock spur of Craigiau Hirion. Here you leave the wall to climb north-west over rocky ground to Craig Llugwy.

Further climbing on this scything spur brings the route in fine fashion to the narrow ridge between Carnedd Llewelyn and Dafydd. Here you look down the length of lonely Cwm Lafar towards Bethesda. Carnedd Dafydd's north-west ridge is dramatic but often in shadow. However, you'll probably be able to make out the sharp rocky Lech Ddu spur above the shadowy Cwmglas Mawr.

Climb left along the stony ridge above the Black Ladders cliffs on easy gradients to reach Carnedd Dafydd's stony summit.

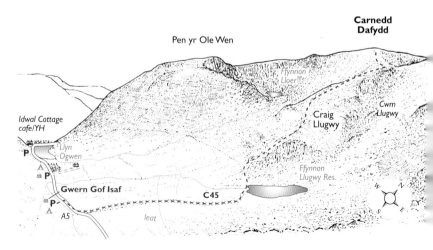

RIDGE ROUTES

Carnedd Llewelyn
Distance: 1¾ miles/3km
Height gain: 460ft/140m
Time: 1 hour

A clearly defined stony path heads east above the spectacular Black Ladders. Beyond Bwlch Cyfrwy-drum the main climb begins up increasingly bouldery terrain to reach the cairn and wind shelters on Carnedd Llewelyn's summit.

Pen yr Ole Wen
Distance: 1¼ miles/2km
Height gain: 410ft/125m
Time: ¾ hour

This very easy passage follows a stony ridge around the enchanting cwm of Ffynnon Lloer before climbing the gentle slopes to Pen yr Ole Wen. It all seems too easy, when you take in the spectacular views of the Glyder and Snowdon mountains seen across the deep defile of Ogwen.

Below: Carnedd Ridge from Dafydd to Pen Yr Ole Wen.

Pen yr Ole Wen, the hill of the white light, soars from the shores of Llyn Ogwen in one steep and savage slope. Its ascent is the cruellest blow in the whole of the great Welsh 3000s expedition, and the descent is nothing less than a violent knee-trembler at the end of many a Carneddau walking day.

Heather and bilberry interspersed with pale rocks are a feature of Pen yr Ole Wen's flanks, adding colour on sunny summer days and a brooding duskiness on the cloudy days of winter. Always, the mountain is a dominant force at Ogwen and Nant Ffrancon where, along with the Glyder peaks from Y Garn to Carnedd y Filiast, it forms the tall walls of a glacial U-shaped valley.

Pen yr Ole Wen's East Ridge is its most splendid feature. Cradling the lake of Ffyn-non Lloer, this rocky spur gives a steep and scrambly but very pleasing route to the top, infinitely superior to the direct Ogwen route.

The summit is a stony one. From it the view back to Tryfan Cwm Idwal and the Glyder peaks is as spectacular as Snowdonia gets, especially on a clear day. To get the best views arrive early or late, as the midday sun often makes everything in that direction a little hazy.

To the north, grassy slopes are drained by three streams whose shallow valleys blur the distinction between the west ridges of Pen yr Ole Wen and those of Carnedd Dafydd. A walker could set out for one peak and change his or her mind halfway through the walk. Braich Ty Du, the ridge overlooking Nant Ffrancon, does however provide a pleasant rambling route of much easier gradients than the Llyn Ogwen approaches.

Opposite: Pen yr Ole Wen towers above Ffynnon Lloer.
Below: Tryfan seen across Pen yr Ole Wen's east ridge.

Route C46
Ogwen Bank and Braich Ty-du
A long plod but with fine views
Start: Lay-by near Ogwen Bank Caravan Park
    (GR: SH 626655)
Distance: 3½ miles/5.5km
Height gain: 2690ft/820m
Time: 2½ hours

From the lay-by follow the road away from Bethesda. A narrow path on the left-hand side of the road begins opposite the entrance lane to the Ogwen Bank Caravan Park and takes the route on a climb through woodland, crossing a gravel forest road before reaching a logging clearing. Turn right here to follow a path to a ladder stile on the edge of open country.

Beyond this the path becomes a green swath through grassy gorse-scattered hillside and heads south-eastwards above a drystone wall. It doubles back left away from the wall, towards the woodland you have just left, but watch out for a narrow zigzag on the right which climbs through more gorse on to the ridge proper. Sheep-tracks lead over the knolls ahead and eventually the wall rejoins the route from the right.

The ridge gets steeper on reaching the bouldery ground of Carreg Fran, and the path meets the main Carneddau ridge at the shallow stony pass of Bwlch yr Ole Wen, where a right turn along an obvious path leads to Pen yr Ole Wen's summit.

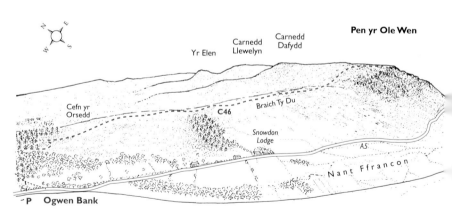

Opposite: Climbing out of Nant Ffrancon on to the Braich Ty-du ridge.

Route C47
Ogwen Cottage and the Direct Ascent
A steep and gruelling route
Start: Idwal Cottage car park
(GR: SH 649603)
Distance: 1¼ miles/2km
Height gain: 2460ft/750m
Time: 1 hour

Route C48
Ogwen Cottage and the East Ridge
The classic mountain route
Start: Glan Dena east of Llyn Ogwen
(GR: SH 668605)
Distance: 4¼ miles/7km
Height gain: 3050ft/930m
Time: 2½ hours

After going through the gap stile in the stone wall to the north of the Afon Ogwen road bridge, the route clambers over a series of rock steps to a grassy shelf where a clear path continues the wickedly steep route though heather and bilberry and crag, then scree. There are stunning retrospective views back across Ogwen to Glyder Fawr, Glyder Fach, Cwm Idwal and Tryfan, whose North Ridge is seen to perfection. Pen yr Ole Wen's convex slopes make false summits inevitable, but the gradient eventually eases to reveal the cairn and wind-shelter on the eastern edge of Pen yr Ole Wen's large stony summit plateau.

Climb the track past the conifers and the cottage of Glan Dena. Where the track turns left for Tal y Llyn farm carry straight on, following a wall northwards to a ladder stile. Beyond this a grass path, waymarked by the odd post, climbs steadily north over ground that is marshy in places. The path is soon joined from the left by the Afon Lloer, which it fords before continuing along the west bank.

After going over the ladder stile in the intake wall there are two choices. You can climb north-west on faint tracks to the bottom of Pen yr Ole Wen's East Ridge (slightly quicker) or you can continue along the main streamside path (recommended). The latter route ends by the shores of Ffynnon Lloer (moon lake), which is set in a magnificent mountain cwm overlooked by the rock slabs of Pen yr Ole Wen and the sweeping grass and stone slopes of Carnedd Dafydd.

By looking left beyond a marshy area you'll locate a boulder slope leading to the base of a huge crag at the foot of the East Ridge. Here, a gully offers an easy scramble

Left: Pen Yr Ole Wen from Ogwen.

134

with good handholds. After that a delightful path climbs the heather-and-crag spur rounding Cwm Lloer. This offers increasingly magnificent views across Ogwen to the Glyderau, where the great cone of Tryfan appears almost as a two-dimensional triangle. The path divides short of Pen yr Ole Wen's summit, the right fork sticking closer to the edge (dangerous when there is snow and ice about). The broad summit has two cairns, one on the very top and one on the Ogwen edge for the best views of Ogwen.

RIDGE ROUTE

Carnedd Dafydd

Distance: 1¼ miles/2km
Height gain: 410ft/125m
Time: ¾ hour

A stony ridge leads unerringly around the cwm of Ffynnon Lloer to Carnedd Dafydd's summit.

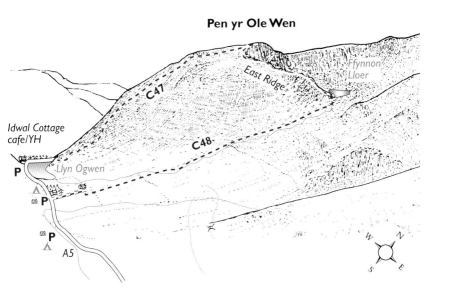

Pen yr Ole Wen

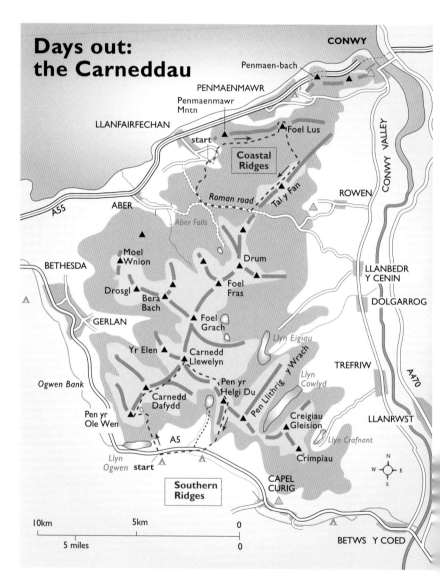

Days out: the Carneddau

CONWY

Penmaen-bach

PENMAENMAWR

Penmaenmawr Mntn

LLANFAIRFECHAN

start

Foel Lus

Coastal Ridges

Roman road

Tal y Fan

ROWEN

CONWY VALLEY

A55

ABER

Aber Falls

Moel Wnion

BETHESDA

Drosgl

Bera Bach

Foel Fras

Drum

Foel Grach

GERLAN

Yr Elen

Carnedd Llewelyn

Ogwen Bank

Pen yr Ole Wen

Carnedd Dafydd

A5

Pen yr Helgi Du

Pen Llithrig y Wrach

Llyn Eigiau

Llyn Cowlyd

Creigiau Gleision

Llyn Crafnant

Crimpiau

LLANBEDR Y CENIN

DOLGARROG

TREFRIW

A470

LLANRWST

Llyn Ogwen   start

Southern Ridges

CAPEL CURIG

N
W — E
S

10km   5km   0

5 miles   0

BETWS Y COED

Days out: the Carneddau

Coastal Ridges

Start: Nant y Coed lower car park
   (GR: SH 695739)
Distance: 12 miles/19km
Height gain: 2390ft/730m
Time: 7–8 hrs

One look at the map reveals that there's a catalogue of Bronze and Iron Age settlements, standing stones, cromlechs and cairns scattered across the whole of the Northern Carneddau. What's more, there's also a Roman road which once linked forts between Chester and Caernarfon. Hopefully, your progress will be less hindered than that of the Romans, who would have been troubled by the Celtic warriors who lived in the hill forts.

The main route begins on the narrow lane, Newry Drive, which doubles back left to climb steeply out of the valley and on to high cow pastures. Ahead now lies Penmaen Mawr (the mountain, not the coastal resort), while to the left beyond Dinas, a domed hill of scree patched with gorse, the bare northern Carneddau stretch across the horizon.

The lane bends left, back towards the coast, but you leave it near the tower of Plas Heulog for a narrow lane on the right. This

Below: The northern Carneddau mountains seen from the track above Llanfairfechan.

Above: The Druids' Circle with Tal y Fan behind.

rakes across the high southern slopes of Pen-maen Mawr. The road ends, but a stony farm track continues through a splendid patch-work of emerald fields and past Blaen-llwyn farm to reach open moorland. North Wales Path waymarkers guide the route eastwards. Tal y Fan and its twin peak, Foel Lwyd, present a ruffled craggy ridge to the south until the rounded grassy hill of Moelfre temporarily shuts them out. Beyond Moelfre, a small path on the right (marked by thin black dashes on the OS Explorer map) leads to the

Druids' Circle, a ring of thirty upright stones. The site actually has nothing to do with the Druids, but is believed to date back to 2100BC.

The path returns to the main track, which comes close to the coastal rim. There's now a view down to the hollow of the resort of Pen-maenmawr, framed by the waves of Conwy Bay and a domed heather hill, Foel Lus.

On reaching the farm pastures of Bryn Derwedd, turn right then left across those pastures to pass the farmhouse. The path continues north-east with a craggy ridge to the left. With the farm of Ty'n-y-ffrith in view, the track arcs left towards Foel Lus. Take the left fork then the next right fork to access the path encircling the heather hill. Below, you'll see two pillars which mark the start of the Jubilee path, opened in 1888 to commemorate the Jubilee of Queen Victoria a year earlier – the path soon joins in from the left. You're now on a splendid balcony route traversing the heather slopes 800ft/244m above sea level. Sea breezes waft in as the constantly changing view opens up to reveal Penmaen Bach, Alltwen and also Conwy Mountain, which lies across the deep hollow of Capelulo and the coastal plains of Dwygyfylch.

After rounding Foel Lus, the path returns to the track you left, just north of Ty'n-y-ffrith.

Keeping the farmhouse well to the lett, go over the ladder stile on the right-hand side of the field before turning left with the North Wales Path to cross the Afon Gyrach on a little footbridge. The path follows the eastern perimeter of more fields before climbing to the ridge north of Cefn Maen Amor. After straddling the ridge the track comes to a tall wall that runs along the high southern flanks. Turn right along a grass track that, in general, follows the course of this wall.

A prominent right fork climbs to the gap between Cefn Maen Amor and Tal y Fan. Leave this for a stony track on the left heading for an old slate mine and its spoil heaps. Keep to the left of the mines and climb the crag-girt slopes leading to Tal y Fan's long ridge. From the summit trig point nearly all of the day's

Below: Llangelynin Church.

route can be traced, while the central Carneddau peaks are lined up on the skyline. It's a big landscape: simple in form, but pleasing in its openness.

The ridge path continues down rocks to the narrow col between Tal y Fan and Foel Lwyd, then over the subsidiary peak and down to the wide pass of Bwlch y Ddeufaen, easily recognised by three lines of pylons which cross the mountains here. A faint path arcs right to cross to the other side of the pass, where it joins the Roman road. Turn right along this wide stony cart track to traverse rough moorland. On reaching a crossroads of tracks, turn right along the one signed Llanfairfechan.

You're now once again following the North Wales Path, this time over Garreg Fawr. After scaling the first grassy summit the path veers left to rake down the west side of the hill. Take the waymarked right fork rather than the track following a wall on the left. This goes through a kissing gate in a cross-wall, then descends to high fields overlooking Nant y Coed. Turn left down a little enclosed ginnel that descends to the road before turning right along the road, which descends further to cross a bridge over the Afon Llanfairfechan. At the other side turn right along the narrow lane back to the car park.

Below: Looking north-east from Tal y Fan's summit.

Southern Ridges

Start: Glan Dena east of Llyn Ogwen
    (GR: SH 668605)
Distance: 9¼ miles/15km
Height gain: 3180ft/970m
Time: 6 hours

Starting from right under Tryfan's North Ridge it seems churlish to face the other way, but there are rewards to come for doing just that. Pen yr Ole Wen might not have the instant appeal of Tryfan, but it is loftier, and what follows will be a delicious promenade on high ridges.

The route begins on a track climbing past the conifer copse and the cottage of Glan Dena. Where the track turns left for Tal y Llyn farm, leave it for the path carrying on up the hill, following a wall northwards to a ladder stile. Beyond this a grass path, waymarked by the odd post, climbs steadily north over ground that can be marshy in places. The tumbling waters of the Afon Lloer should be forded before continuing along the west bank. Its course should be traced to the shores of Ffynnon Lloer (moon lake). The situation is stunning, for the cwm is enclosed by the crags of Pen yr Ole Wen's East Ridge and the vast stony flanks of Carnedd Dafydd.

The route will now tackle that East Ridge. To find the start of the path, look left across a marshy area to locate the bouldery slope leading to the base of a huge crag at the foot of the ridge. There's an easy scramble with good handholds up a gulley, above which a delightful path continues the climb on the

heather-and-crag spur that traces the rim of Cwm Lloer. As the path nears the summit, the views back to Ogwen become more spectacular, with Tryfan appearing as a thin wedge of crag and Cwm Idwal as a gigantic shadowy hollow, lined by huge crags.

Above: Carneddau ponies.

Where the path divides just short of Pen yr Ole Wen's broad stony summit, take the left fork which aims for the summit cairns – there's one on the very top and one on the Ogwen edge for the best views of Ogwen.

Continuing from the top, the path dips very slightly to the shallow pass of Bwlch yr Ole Wen before climbing steadily north-east along the bouldery ridge to Carnedd Dafydd's summit. It heads east from the summit, hugging the edge above the spectacular Black Ladders (the Ysgolion Duon cliffs), which hide from the sun and plummet hundreds of feet into the lonely wastelands of Cwm Llafar.

Beyond the pass of Bwlch Cyfrwy-drum, the main climb begins up increasingly bouldery terrain towards the huge rounded summit of Carnedd Llewelyn. Looking back, the craggy Lech Du ridge and the bouldery Cwm-glas Bach now dominate Cwm Llafar. These climbing and scrambling grounds have now overtaken the Black Ladders in popularity.

After crossing increasingly bouldery ground, the route attains the cairn and wind shelters on Carnedd Llewelyn's summit. Because of its vastness, the views from Llewelyn's summit plateau are limited, but by going to the rims you will be able to look into several rocky cwms. Both Cwm Lloer (west) and Cwm Llyffant (east) have small tarns in them.

Now head ESE across the stony plateau to locate the ridge overlooking the little lake of Ffynnon Lyffant. The route continues over easier ground to Craig yr Ysfa where you look down the spectacular Amphitheatre and its immense crags. Cwm Eigiau lies far below, another lonely Carneddau valley which in times gone by would have echoed to the sounds of Bronze Age tribes, then later to those of hundreds of quarrymen.

A short craggy section requires caution, especially in wintry conditions when the slippery rock can be treacherous. The path descends further to Bwlch Eryl Farchog.

Below: Climbing high on Pen yr Ole Wen's east ridge.

Ahead lies Pen yr Helgi Du and a short, steep path clambering over crags interspersed with bilberry and heather. Although it's not too serious, under normal conditions most walkers will need a steadying hand on the rocks.

In sharp contrast, Pen yr Helgi Du's summit is grassy, but a walk to the northern edge reveals vegetated cliffs overlooking Cwm Eigiau. The views back to Craig yr Ysfa and its Amphitheatre are memorable, and backed up by Carnedd Llewelyn's stony east flanks.

You're on the home run now. Just head down the southern spur of Y Braich. The route is a tonic for tired limbs and the wide views of the Glyder mountains are soothing on the

eyes. At the bottom of the ridge there's a ladder stile over a fence, then a bridge over a water leat. A faint path, marked with black dashes on the OS Explorer map, angles half-left down rough pastures above Tal y Braich farm to meet a stony track, which continues the descent to the A5 road.

Across the road another track heads south past conifers, crossing footbridges over a minor stream, then the Afon Llugwy, to meet a bridleway track that runs along the length of Nant y Benglog. Turn right along it to pass both Gwern y Gof farms before returning to the A5 opposite Glan Dena and the start of the walk.

Below: Gallt yr Ogof from the east Glyderau ridge.

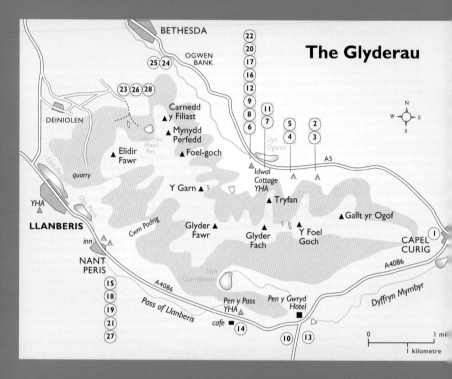

2. The Glyderau

The name Glyder comes from the Celtic word *cludr*, which means a rock pile. This is a very apt description because the cwms and spiky ridges of the two main peaks, Glyder Fawr and Glyder Fach, however impressive, are laid out in random fashion. Seen from Ogwen, the big two Glyderau have none of the classic mountain architecture of Snowdon, nor do they have the well-rounded smoothness of the Carneddau. The day is saved by Tryfan, a lower triangle of a mountain boasting colossal buttresses on its east face.

THE PEAKS

Main Tops	height	
Glyder Fawr	3279ft	999m
Glyder Fach	3262ft	994m
Y Garn	3106ft	947m
Elidir Fawr	3031ft	924m
Tryfan	3002ft	915m
Foel-goch	2726ft	831m
Carnedd y Filiast	2694ft	821m
Mynydd Perfedd	2664ft	812m
Y Foel Goch	2641ft	805m
Gallt yr Ogof	2503ft	763m

In reality it's the sheer ruggedness of the Glyder range that appeals – Snowdon just cannot compete on this score. The Glyderau offer more sport per metre than anywhere else in Wales. The cliffs and arêtes, too numerous to mention, are heaven-sent for walkers, scramblers and climbers alike, and the bouldery summit plateaux offer many attractions: the jagged ramparts of the Castle of the Winds; the Cantilever, where you can 'walk the plank', and Bristly Ridge, which offers the intermediate walker and scrambler a stiff test, but is not so daunting that they dare not complete it.

Ogwen is a special place, where the great peaks of the Carneddau and Glyderau meet and squeeze civilization into a sliver of land where there's just enough room for Thomas Telford's A5 highway to Holyhead and a handful of cottages, which include an outdoor centre, a youth hostel and a café. Above Ogwen lies the cliff-hung hollow of Idwal, with its lake, climbing slabs and the rocky declivity of the Devil's Kitchen.

It has been said that Idwal is the haunt of demons. Eighteenth-century writer Thomas Pennant wrote that it was 'a place to inspire murderous thoughts, environed with horrible precipices', and it was here that legend states that Idwal, son of Owain Gwynedd, was brutally murdered. On a day when the mists mingle with the shadows of crags, and when rain-enhanced waterfalls fall out from those mists, you can still experience that menace.

The roadside Ogwen waterfalls are spectacular after rain. Here the river tumbles in white-water torrents down giant crags and boulders to the U-shaped valley and green fields of Nant Ffrancon. It's here that the Glyder range bends northwards to form the shape of a boomerang, and from here that a certain amount of that randomness disappears, replaced by steep-sided ridges with several cliff-ringed hanging valleys.

Y Garn is the most eminent of these, displaying a powerful presence, but Foelgoch's precipitous crags and pointed summit are a good second. These Nant Ffrancon flanks have few recognizable paths and are not often climbed from here. But intrepid walkers will discover secretive places and shady corners, tiny pools, dusky heather spurs and empty ridges – they might even discover my lost Garmin eTrex Vista GPS receiver too!

That brings us to Ogwen Bank, just short of Bethesda. Here the Glyderau end in ignominy. Slate slag, piled high on to mountainside terraces, forms the skyline above both Llanberis and Bethesda. Elidir Fawr and Carnedd y Filiast have had ridges exploded off them: they look like war victims with lost limbs. At Cwm Marchlyn, between the two peaks, the quarries almost meet but the power-hungry electricity men beat them to the land when they constructed a pump-storage power station, with Cwm Marchlyn being dammed to form the top reservoir. The power station itself is built deep into the mountain's core. Proudly, they call this the Electric Mountain.

It has often been said that the Glyderau are grassy in the south, but this is an oversimplification. Seen from Capel Curig or Pen y Gwryd, the Glyderau are simpler in form, with expansive slopes of heather, boulders and outcrops rising to those ridgeline castles. On these slopes lies Dyffryn Mymbyr, a farmhouse that was once home to Thomas Firbank, who in 1938 broke the record for the Welsh 3000s, run in just

Above: Shafts of sunlight break through the clouds, adding a little drama to Tryfan's magnificent eastern buttresses.

under 8½ hours. Colin Donnelly's present-day record of 4 hours 19.56 minutes puts the run in perspective, but Firbank did write a fascinating account in *I Bought a Mountain* – a darned good read for evenings spent in the tent or the hostel. Even if you're too unfit to run the Welsh 3000s, the book will still let you know how to round up and shear sheep.

At the Llanberis Pass, between Snowdon and the Glyderau, everything changes. The Glyder get serious with the steely-grey climbers' crags of Dinas y Gromlech overlooking a massive jumble of boulder, crag and scree. Glyder Fawr makes a defiant stand with its Esgair Felen ridge before giving way to the greenery of Y Garn's southern slopes and Nant Peris. This is more gentle scenery, with long moorland cwms stretching towards the main ridge. Many of the paths on the maps don't exist on the ground here, but once you leave the low pastures behind you're in the access areas and are free to roam – a far better prospect than heavily engineered tracks.

Gallt yr Ogof, the steep slope of the cave, is the most easterly of the Glyder peaks, the one you see on the A5 after your bacon sandwich and steaming cup of tea at Capel Curig's Pinnacle Café. It's one hulk of a hill, with steep cliffs overlooking a wide marshy cwm formed by two watercourses, the Nant y Gors and the Afon Bwlch Goleuni. In fact, Gallt yr Ogof looks like Tryfan with the top buttresses and that distinctive cockscomb summit profile chopped off. The cave can be seen quite clearly from the A5. It's cut into those cliffs to the left of a prominent scree gully.

Most walkers visit Gallt yr Ogof on their way along the ridge from Capel Curig to Glyders Fawr and Fach. Many of these probably bypass the mountaintop too, as the ridge path cuts below the summit rocks. The ridge *is* the best way: it's easier and offers good views all along the way, but for those who like a little excitement, the previously mentioned scree gully gets you among those fearsome cliffs and shows you the way to the mountain's heart. The views too are worth the climb. Llyn Cowlyd can be seen squatting uneasily between the shaly slopes of Pen yr Llithrig y Wrach and the rock-and-heather knolls of Creigiau Gleision, while Tryfan's eastern buttresses and Glyder Fach's jagged Bristly Ridge are seen to their best advantage across two heathery cwms.

Opposite: Gallt yr Ogof from the upper Llugwy Valley.
Below: Glyder Fach and Tryfan from the summit of Gallt yr Ogof.

Route G1
Capel Curig

A fine ridge route with good views from start to finish

Start: Car park behind Pinnacle Café, Capel Curig (GR: SH 720582)

Distance: 2½ miles/4km

Height gain: 1940ft/590

Time: 1½ hours

The walk starts on the northbound cart track at the back of the car park and leads gently into the valley of the Llugwy. Just beyond Gelli farm leave the track for an indistinct path climbing between rocky bluffs on to the grassy Glyder ridge. From here, early views include the Llugwy valley slinking away beneath the sullen grasslands of Pen yr Llithrig y Wrach and Pen yr Helgi Du, while in the opposite direction the twin lakes of Mymbyr shelter beneath the barren slopes of Moel Siabod.

Above: Gallt yr Ogof seen across the Llugwy Valley.

By the time the route reaches Cefn y Capel, a path of sorts has established itself, mostly on the southern side of the ridge, but occasionally popping to the top to see if the Carneddau are still there.

The great dark cliffs of Gallt yr Ogof glower across a wide plateau, but the path you're on stays to the south of the summit. However, getting to the summit is only a matter of clambering up a few boulders.

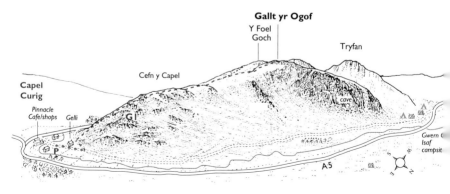

Route G2
The North Ridge

A stiff gully climb, but the best route to the top

Start: Gwern Gof Isaf camp site car park near Capel Curig (pay at farm)
(GR: SH 686602)
Distance: 1½ miles /2.5km
Height gain: 1610ft/490
Time: 1 hour

Note: The gully isn't pleasant in descent

After going up the drive to the farmhouse of Gwern Gof Isaf, head east on the cart track which was once the main road through the valley. Gallt yr Ogof's bold ramparts are directly ahead. It passes the stand of pines and runs parallel to the Afon Llugwy. It then crosses the Nant yr Ogof stream and tucks under the cliffs of Gallt yr Ogof.

Leave the track and head for the prominent gully slanting between those cliffs. You'll see the cave in those cliffs to the left of the route. The lower slopes are steep and bouldery but soon the cliffs close in. The best route hugs the cliffs on the left, from where a scramble up scree and boulders brings the route to the top of the crags. The views across the face of Y Foel Goch to Tryfan and the Glyder Fach's Bristly Ridge make the efforts of the gully worthwhile, as the route continues along the crag and heather of the north ridge for just over a half mile to the summit.

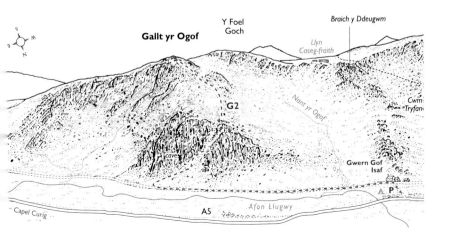

151

Other route options

There are several quite unpleasant or point-
less routes to the top. You could trace Nant yr
Ogof to the col between Y Foel Goch and
Gallt yr Ogof. For those who like wet tussocky ground, the wide hollow of Nant y
Gors will provide it. A grassy rake to the east
of the crags takes this route to the mountain's
east ridge.

RIDGE ROUTES

Y Foel Goch

Distance: ¼ mile/1km
Height gain: 280ft/ 85m
Time: 25–30 minutes

Descend westwards along the craggy ridge to
the grassy col in between to join the main
path, which veers right of a small pool and its
marshy surrounds. Ignore the path where it
rounds Y Foel Goch on the left and just aim
for the crags of the summit.

Right: Gallt yr Ogof from the north.

Known as the Unnamed Peak until somebody decided that it would be called Y Foel Goch, the red bare hill. This is confusing as there's a Foel-goch on the same ridge – but I suppose such a big hill merits a real name. More poetically it could have been called Carn Caseg-fraith (the cairn of the piebald mare), linking it with the shallow pools and cwm of Caseg-fraith.

Y Foel Goch is an unremarkable peak which is overshadowed in almost every way by its next-door neighbours, Tryfan and Glyder Fach. However, it has in Braich y Ddeugwm one of the best little spurs in the range: grassy, but with just enough rock to scramble over to make things exciting. I suppose I could say the mountain has its own tarn, Llyn Caseg-fraith, but it would be stretching a point to call these peat pools and their squelchy surrounds tarns – and Glyder Fach may also have a claim to them.

The usual hard rock of the Glyderau crowns the summit and forms squat cliffs along the northern edge, and there's just enough grass between them to offer splendid resting places. Very few walkers make Y Foel Goch their prime objective, but the mountain has its own charm. If you want a place to chill out, away from the crowds, this is for you.

Opposite: Y Foel Goch across Cwm Tryfan.

Route G3
Braich y Ddeugwm
A stairway to heaven
Start: Gwern Gof Isaf car park (charge)
   (GR: SH 685603)
Distance: 2½ miles/ 4km
Height gain: 1740ft/ 530m
Time: 1½ hours

After going down the farm drive, turn right along the bridleway track, whose gate is signed Caseg Ffraith, then immediately left at the base of the rocks to locate the ladder stile on the right-hand side of the farmhouse. The rock bluffs of Braich y Ddeugwm now provide a glorious stairway to the skyline. Keep initially to the western side to locate a stile straddling a fence. Beyond that it is best to keep to the crest, where the route, a combination of grassy paths, small rushy pools and smooth slabby outcrops, climbs between Cwm Tryfan and Cwm Gwern Gof. It affords truly memorable views of Tryfan across its wild heathery cwm.

The gradient eases as Llyn Caseg-fraith is reached. A sketchy track passes through the marshy surrounds to the north of the shallow tarn and its tiny attendant pools. After rising to the head of Cwm Tryfan, the path meets the Miners' Track that links Ogwen and Pen y Gwryd. Here you turn left (east) on a narrow path climbing towards Y Foel Goch. The main path skirts the southern side, but a left fork takes you to the top.

Route G4
Cwm Tryfan

*A historic path through a wild
heathery cwm*

Start: Gwern Gof Uchaf (GR: SH 673608)
Distance: 2½ miles/4km
Height gain: 1640ft/ 500m
Time: 1½ hours

The Miners' Track from Gwern Gof Uchaf, which climbs through the heather and crags of Cwm Tryfan, offers a fine alternative which is always in the shadow of Tryfan. Go up the drive to Gwern Gof Uchaf farm and campsite and keep the farmhouse to the right. Follow the path SSW, keeping to the right of Tryfan Bach, a pyramid of good climbing rock aping its somewhat bigger neighbour. Ignore paths to the right, which aim for Tryfan and Heather Terrace. There's a steep pitched section of path taking the route into the heathery Cwm Tryfan.

You'll hear the chatter from walkers on Heather Terrace, which rakes across the buttresses of Tryfan above you, and the splashes of Nant Gwern y Gof to the left, but otherwise all is quiet in this shady rock-and-heather cwm. As the path gains height, the pinnacles of Bristly Ridge peep out from the horizon ahead. After a slightly downhill section, the stony path that has brought us so far degenerates into a steep boulder run, but the difficulties are short-lived as this takes you to the Miners' Track, which traverses the upper cwm from Bwlch Tryfan. Turn left along this and follow it up to the grassy col just west of the shallow pools of Llyn Caseg-fraith. Watch out for the path on the left, which crosses marshy ground before climbing to Y Foel Goch. Take the left fork just below the summit as in Route G3.

Below: Miners' Track, Cwm Tryfan.

Other route options

The obvious one, and it's a good one, is the Miners' Track from Pen y Gwryd, a pleasant route over rock and heather slopes (see Route G10 to Glyder Fach). The route would meet Routes G3/4 at Llyn Caseg-fraith.

RIDGE ROUTES

Above: On the summit rocks of Y Foel Goch.

Gallt yr Ogof

Distance: ¼ mile/1km
Height gain: 130ft/40m
Time: 20–30 minutes

Descend eastwards down grass-and-rock slopes to the col where you rejoin the main ridge path which has come in from the right. This keeps to the left of some marshy ground. As the path starts to round Galt yr Ogof on the right, leave it for a direct ascent to the craggy top.

Glyder Fach

Distance: 1½ miles/2.5km
Height gain: 820ft/250m
Time: ¾–1 hour

Descend north to the grassy col south of the pools of Caseg-fraith. A peaty path becomes increasingly stony as it climbs the ridge at the head of Cwm Tryfan. Eventually the route clambers over boulder slopes to attain the fascinating summit of spiky rocks and huge outcrops.

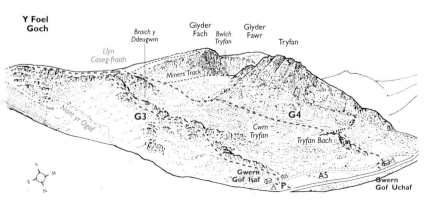

157

Tryfan, whose name means three summits, is the most distinctively shaped mountain in Wales, as recognisable as Ben Nevis and as shapely as Stac Polly. It's triangular in shape, almost two-dimensional, and has a serrated top rather like a cockscomb. Even though at around 3002ft/915m it is considerably lower than its neighbours, Tryfan lords it over the Llugwy Valley, rising from the waters of Llyn Ogwen to its summit in savage simplicity. There are no complex ridges and cwms, just one rock crest soaring to the skies. Glyder Fawr and Glyder Fach languish in the shadowy backstage of Idwal and Bochlwyd.

Tryfan has two faces: east and west. The east face rises from the sullen heathery hollow of Cwm Tryfan and has several near vertical buttresses neatly divided by the blackness of deep gulleys and skirted by a seemingly near-perfect ledge, known as Heather Terrace – but this perfection isn't quite matched by reality when you're clambering over the jumbled rocks of the terrace.

The west face is gentler in comparison but perhaps even more chaotic, with a rounded grassy shoulder rising from Ogwen to three

Opposite: Tryfan's west face towers above Llyn Ogwen.

quarters of the way to the main summit. The shoulder is protected by rock and scree on two sides, but walkers could keep their hands in their pockets until reaching the rock face, which hereabouts is a mix of loose scree and shattered rocks. At the bottom of the west face, the Milestone Buttress was first scaled at the turn of the 19th century by climbing pioneer O. G. Jones.

The simplicity of Tryfan's contours means that there are only a handful of walkers' routes. All require the use of hands, if only for steadying. But this belligerent-looking peak is a more friendly soul than it at first appears. True, the slopes are steep, but mostly the rock is solid with good handholds. And there's a surprising amount of vegetation. Even on the North Ridge scramble there are shelves and corners lush with bilberry and heather.

Tryfan's great presence and its exciting scrambles mean that it is the most climbed of the Welsh peaks after Snowdon. In summer, if you don't want to queue at every difficult crag, start early, start very early.

Below: Mist swirls around Tryfan's east face.

Route G5

Heather Terrace

A fine route beneath the spectacular
*   buttresses of the east face*

Start: Roadside parking, Gwern Gof Uchaf
   (GR: SH 673605)

Distance: 2 miles/3km

Height gain: 2000ft/610m

Time: 1–1½ hours

From a distance Heather Terrace looks like a
clearly defined ledge angling across the spectacular east face of Tryfan. First-time visitors
to the mountain will be surprised to find that
it's nowhere near as obvious when close at
hand. The route involves a small amount of
easy scrambling, as all routes up Tryfan do,
but nothing serious in good weather conditions. It's a spectacular route, probably the
best one for those not ready to tackle the
North Ridge.

From the A5, go up the drive of Gwern Gof
Uchaf. Keeping the farmhouse to the right, go
over the stile on to the old road, now a cart
track. Turn right along this to the next ladder
stile on the left. From this a paved path climbs
towards Tryfan's great eastern buttresses. The
path passes to the right of Tryfan Bach, a
model-sized Tryfan popular with novice
climbers – you'll see why when you view the
diagonal crags of its west face from above.

On reaching the wall don't go over the stile
but turn right alongside it. This path soon
climbs steeply towards a low shoulder on

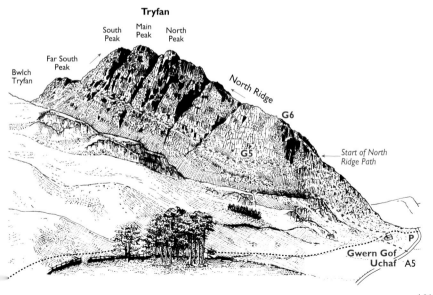

Tryfan's crest. Just before reaching the top watch out for a small path on the left– this is the beginning of Heather Terrace. (Note: don't go all the way to the crest or you'll find yourself on the North Ridge scramble.)

The route, mostly clear on the ground, is a mix of stony paths through the heather, bilberry and rock, and simple scrambles over low crags and outcrops. Often there is more than one option. In the higher stages you'll find yourself mixing with climbers tackling those mighty buttresses. The dusky heather grounds of Cwm Tryfan are far below, bound by the rocks of Foel Goch and Braich y Ddeugwm.

High up the terrace, the path divides. The left fork descends towards Bwlch Tryfan before climbing a scree path to the South Ridge. The right fork, an infinitely better course, soon starts a short scramble over boulders towards the South Ridge. You'll see one of two ladder stiles on a grassy col ahead (it's between the Far South and South Peaks and marked on the OS map by the 850m spot height), but there's a steep drop over crags at first. Avoid this by continuing the scramble to the right and you'll come to the second stile (20m to the right of the first).

Now the clamber up the South Ridge begins. Go over the stile before climbing right on a stony path climbing to a col between the South and Main summits. A short climb brings you to the Main Summit, where you'll find walkers congregating around the monoliths known as Adam and Eve.

Opposite: The path climbing above Gwern Gof Uchaf.
Below: Heather Terrace.

Route G6
The North Ridge

A spectacular route straight up the nose of
*   Wales's most distinctive mountain*
Start: Llyn Ogwen (GR: SH 673605)
Distance: 1 mile/1.5km
Height gain: 2000ft/610m
Time: 1–1½ hours

Note: A Grade 1 scramble (Grade 2 if the
direct route is taken up the steep tower
above the Cannon). Not suitable for walkers
during poor or wintry conditions

Although the North Ridge is unerringly steep with countless gulleys and rock-faces, there is no one true way up. The difficulties can often be bypassed and the scratches of boots on the rock are always a comforting guide to keeping you on course for the top.

From the back of the lay-by car park just west of the foot of Tryfan's North Ridge, go through the kissing gate and climb steeply to the foot of a great wall of climbing crag, known as the Milestone Buttress due to its proximity to the milestone on the A5 lay-by opposite. Skirt left around the base of the crags and on to the shoulder of Tryfan. The path on the ridge begins with a scree run and continues with a plethora of paths tackling the boot-polished crags of the narrowing ridge. Stay close to the crest, but if anywhere looks particularly hard, there will almost certainly be an easier and obvious route somewhere nearby. This advice applies to the whole route.

Below: On Adam and Eve, on Tryfan's main summit.
Opposite: On Tryfan's North Ridge (photograph by Roy Clayton).

Eventually you'll come to a short level section banded with white quartz. Just around the corner on the right is the Cannon, a prominent, tilted rock pillar seemingly ready to fire across Ogwen. Back on the main path the continuing route climbs quite steeply to a long sloping grassy shoulder, at the end of which there is often a queue waiting to tackle a tower of rock – this, although solid, is polished and requires a cautious ascent before dropping down to the Notch. This is a Grade 2 scramble; an easier alternative from the cairn at the base of this final tower (GR 665 596) descends left through a gap in the rocks and continues out to and around the eastern face of the mountain. The slanting path reaches a gully blocked by a chockstone boulder. Scramble a few metres to the right of it to enter the gully. There's a jammed boulder to negotiate at the top of the gully. Above this you reach the Notch.

Now there's just a delightful scramble to the North Summit, where a boulder ridge drops to a small col just a short clamber from Adam and Eve on the Main Summit.

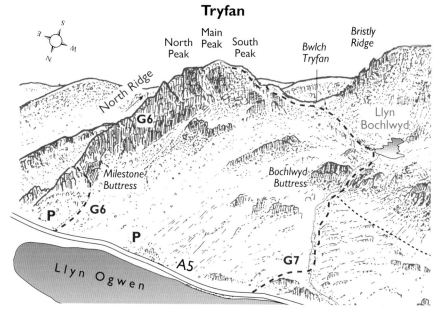

Tryfan

North Peak · Main Peak · South Peak · Bwlch Tryfan · Bristly Ridge · North Ridge · G6 · Milestone Buttress · Llyn Bochlwyd · Bochlwyd Buttress · G6 · P · P · A5 · G7 · Llyn Ogwen

Route G7
Llyn Bochlwyd

A stimulating route past waterfalls, crags and a fine glacial cwm

Start: A5 roadside car park opposite Llyn Ogwen (GR: SH 656602)

Distance: 1½ miles /2.5km

Height gain: 2030ft/620m

Time: 1½ hours

Beyond the ladder stile at the back of the car park a pitched path climbs steeply up a rocky bank. The path soon becomes intermittent as it heads south-west over undulating grassland towards the Bochlwyd stream, which it fords above a waterfall. The path maintains direction to meet the paved Miners' Track, where a left turn is made to reach a steep section climbing to the outflow of Llyn Bochlwyd. Cross the stream on the flat section by the tarn. This is a fine location with the grey rock walls and boulder slopes of Glyder Fach soaring to its serrated skyline, and Tryfan looking its rugged best to the left. A sometimes stony, sometimes paved, path climbs towards Bwlch Tryfan, the wide and deep saddle between the two mountains.

Where the path divides some 400m below the saddle take the left fork, which skirts the crags of the Far South Top to arrive at a wall running along a grassy col (850m spot height). Ignore the two ladder stiles in the wall and instead continue up a stony path that winds up the rocks of the South Ridge. The path reaches the narrow gap between the South and Main Summits. A short clamber over boulder and rock leads to Adam and Eve on the Main Summit.

Other route options

Standing by the shores of Llyn Ogwen, you can see an eroded path climbing straight up the middle of a grassy spur beneath Tryfan's main summits. This route is feasible and used as a descent route on the Welsh 3000s. However, it is neither pleasant (steep with loose rocks high on the west face) nor is it aesthetically sustainable, and I really cannot bring myself to recommend it. Another possibility is to take the Cwm Tryfan track from Gwern Gof Uchaf beneath the east face and follow it to Bwlch Tryfan, from where you can gain the South Ridge.

Above: Tryfan seen across Llyn Bochlwyd.

RIDGE ROUTE

Glyder Fach

Distance: 1 mile/1.5km
Height gain: 880ft/ 270m
Time: 1 hour

Descend the worn rocky path down the south ridge, passing to the right of the two ladder stiles at the top of the Heather Terrace route, before descending on an obvious path to Bwlch Tryfan. From here there are two choices:

1. Go over either of two ladder stiles in the wall on the left and follow the loose scree path to the left of Bristly Ridge.
2. Keep the wall along the saddle to the left before breaking off half-right over a scree slope to a prominent gully at the foot of Bristly Ridge. Climb the gully including the boulder blocking the entrance – the steep upper section is the hardest of the whole route. Here the broken rocky ground on the right is the easiest way to gain the crest, where scratches on the rock highlight the way over the exposed ups and downs of the pinnacled ridge. Suddenly you come to the gap beyond the Great Pinnacle, a seemingly insurmountable notch. There *is* a direct descent, however, and the route continues right to left through the gap and takes a gently angled groove to the left of a steep tower. This leads back to the crest, where the scrambling ends. After a shallow dip the ridge leads to the bouldery summit plateau of Glyder Fach, not far from the Cantilever and a short way east of the summit rock-pile.

Below: On the south ridge of Tryfan above Bwlch Tryfan.

Above: Castell y Gwynt, castle of the winds.

The small rock-pile – that's what the name Glyder Fach means – is a mere 17ft/5m lower than Glyder Fawr, the big rock-pile. Like most small relations, Glyder Fach has to work harder for recognition, and it does this admirably. The mountain's north-west face displays typical ruggedness, with its crags known simply as the Main Cliff.

At first glance it is a jumble of broken rock strewn across very steep flanks, but closer inspection shows there are solid rock buttresses and pillars. Unfortunately these are the preserve of climbers, but there are good opportunities nearby for the walker and scrambler because Glyder Fach's summit is a fairground of rock features, with little room for grass.

Approaching the summit from the east the first feature you'll come across is the Cantilever, a gigantic horizontal slab of rock perched precariously on a couple of vertical outcrops – usually you'll have to queue up to pose for the mandatory 'walking the plank' picture. Nearby, some spiky rocks teeter on the precipitous northern edge. On further inspection you'll see that these are the top rocks of a jagged spur, Bristly Ridge, which plummets down to Bwlch Tryfan like a dragon's tail – it's a fine Grade 1 scramble. To the east of this is a loose, zigzagging scree path.

A huge mound of boulder and crag tops Glyder Fach's summit, but further west you'll find the mountain's most fascinating feature – the romantically named Castell y Gwynt, castle of the winds. Often in shadow, this castle is a powerful rampart of serrated rock-spears, guarding Bwlch y Ddwy Glyder, the wild pass dividing Glyder Fach from its big brother, Glyder Fawr.

Route G8

The Miners' Track: Cwm Bochlwyd and Glyder Fach

An ancient track used by the copper miners of Snowdon

Start: Idwal Cottage car park
  (GR: SH 649603)
Distance: 2¼ miles/5km
Height gain: 2800ft/850m
Time: 2 hours

Follow the Cwm Idwal path from the left of the toilet block, leaving it at the first big right-hand bend. Here the partially paved Miners' Track heads south-east, across marshy ground at first, beneath the rocks of Clogwyn y Tarw, then into the hollow of Nant Bochlwyd. There's a very steep section as the stepped path climbs by the rocky terrain of Llyn Bochlwyd's outflow stream to enter Cwm Bochlwyd. Here the large tarn is stunningly sited beneath Tryfan's western walls, the rocky spur of Y Cribin and Glyder Fach, where the upthrusts of Bristly Ridge, the summit and the Castle of the Winds top a near-vertical and often shadowed rock-face.

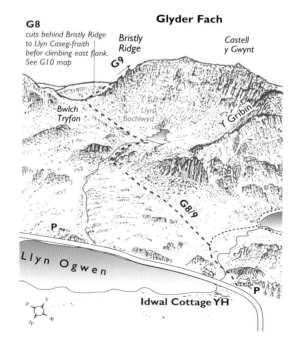

Glyder Fach

G8
cuts behind Bristly Ridge to Llyn Caseg-fraith befor climbing east flank. See G10 map

Bristly Ridge

Castell y Gwynt

G9

Bwlch Tryfan

Llyn Bochlwyd

Y Cribin

G8/9

P

L l y n O g w e n

P

Idwal Cottage YH

The path continues along the east side of Llyn Bochlwyd, climbing to Bwlch Tryfan, a high pass between Tryfan and Glyder Fach's Bristly Ridge. On the other side there's a slight drop as the path rounds the head of Cwm Tryfan, a wild peat-and-heather hollow reminiscent of the Scottish Highlands. The path comes to the main Glyder ridge just short of the shallow pools of Llyn Caseg-fraith. It now turns right across grassland, roughly following the edge, before veering left. Leave this cairned path for a faint path climbing up the stone-and-grass slopes of Glyder Fach. Further up the path frequently loses itself in boulder-fields but finds itself again on the gravelly sections. It reaches the summit plateau between the spiky rocks that crown Bristly Ridge and those of the Cantilever.

Below: Bristly Ridge seen from Bwlch Tryfan, showing the path gently curving to the right away from the wall towards the bottom of the gully that is used to gain the ridge.

Route G9
Bristly Ridge Alternative

A Grade 1 scramble up a pinnacled arête

Start: Idwal Cottage car park
  (GR: SH 649603)
Distance: 2¼ miles (5km)
Height gain: 2800ft/850m
Time: 2½ hours

The Grade 1 scramble up Bristly Ridge makes an exhilarating approach to Glyder Fach. Most of the steepest sections can be avoided but, for the most part, keep close to the crest. Polished rock and boot-scratches make complex route descriptions unnecessary.

Follow Route G8 to the cross-wall on Bwlch Tryfan. Keep the wall along the saddle to the left before breaking off half-right over a scree slope to a prominent gully at the foot of Bristly Ridge. Climb the gully including the boulder blocking the entrance – the steep upper section is the hardest of the whole route. Here, the broken rocky ground on the right is the easiest way to gain the crest, where scratches on the rock highlight the way over the exposed pinnacled ridge.

Suddenly you come to the gap beyond the Great Pinnacles, a seemingly insurmountable notch. There *is* a direct descent, however, and the route continues right to left through the gap and takes a gently angled groove to the left of a steep tower. This leads back to the crest, where the scrambling ends. After a shallow dip the ridge leads to the bouldery summit plateau of Glyder Fach, not far from the Cantilever, east of the summit rock-pile.

Route G10
Pen y Gwryd and the Miners' Track

An ancient track used by the copper miners of Snowdon

Start: Llyn Lockwood, Pen y Gwryd (GR: SH 662559)

Distance: 2¼ miles/ 3.5km

Height gain: 2400ft/730m

Time: 1½ hours

The path begins at a roadside ladder stile across the road from the lay-by car park and crosses marshy grassland. A footbridge straddles the lively stream of Nant Gwryd and the ground gradually steepens, heading northeast. It's easy to see the path as it cuts across the heather and boulders diagonally south to the skyline. In late summer the heather pro-vides a colourful foreground to the wide southern vista, which includes Moel Siabod, Cnicht and the Moelwyns, separated from the Snowdon group by the curving Gwynant valley. One of Snowdon's finest façades – Crib-goch, Yr Wyddfa and Crib-y-ddysgl – towers over the rugged Llanberis Pass, displaying the reddish hues that give rise to the name Crib-goch, red ridge. This is fine coffee-stop territory – and you can dip your toes in the nearby stream too.

The ground becomes firmer as the path starts climbing those slopes in earnest, passing beneath an attractive waterfall before reaching the grass of the ridge. Just short of Llyn y Caseg-fraith, a cairned path turns left to climb the bouldery east flanks of Glyder Fach as in Route G8.

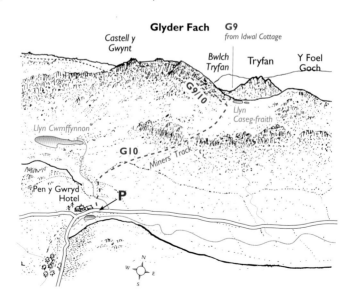

Glyder Fach G9
from Idwal Cottage

Castell y Gwynt

Bwlch Tryfan   Tryfan   Y Foel Goch

G9/10

Llyn Caseg-fraith

Llyn Cwmffynnon

G10   Miners' Track

Pen y Gwryd Hotel

P

Other route options

Those who like scrambling might like to divert from Route G8 at Llyn Bochlwyd to tackle the Gribin ridge (see Route G11, Glyder Fawr). This would bring you to the Glyder Fawr ridge just west of the pass of Bwlch y Ddwy Glyder. Take the path on the left down to the pass, then the one keeping to the right side of Castell y Gwynt. Climb the boulder field to gain the Glyder Fach plateau.

RIDGE ROUTES

Glyder Fawr

Distance: 1 mile/1.5km
Height gain: 260ft/80m
Time: ¾ hour

Head west towards Castell y Gwynt, then follow a descending path to the left. Where the path ends, scramble down the boulder fields ahead to reach the pass of Bwlch y Ddwy Glyder, where a gradual climb along a cairned path takes you on to Glyder Fawr's summit.

Y Foel Goch

Distance: 1½ miles/2.5km
Height gain: 210ft/65m
Time: 1 hour

From the pile of stones on the summit head east to pass between the Cantilever and the spiky top rocks of Bristly Ridge. From here scramble down the boulder fields, with the shallow pools of Llyn Caseg-fraith sheltering in the grassy pass below. On reaching the pass, cut across the Miners' Track. Following a narrow path that passes to the right of the pools, take the left fork on the slopes beyond. This leads to the rocky crown of Y Foel Goch.

Left: Crossing Nant Gwryd near the start of Route G10, with Glyder Fach behind.

173

GLYDER FAWR

Glyder Fawr, the big pile of stones, is, as the name suggests, the highest of the Glyder range. Like Glyder Fach, the summit is a bit of a moonscape, a jumble of boulders scattered with spiky rock outcrops. However, Glyder Fawr's summit plateau is smooth by comparison: the boulders are smaller and, more often than not, provide an easy walking surface.

Although there's no regimented architecture, the components that go to make a great mountain are all there. Pride of Glyder Fawr are its glacial cwms and rocky arêtes. Cwm Idwal is the largest of the cwms and was designated a National Nature Reserve in 1954.

At the back of the cwm and its large tarn there's a mysteriously dark defile, where a column of basalt divides the mountainside's volcanic bedrock. Known as Twll Du or the Devil's Kitchen, it was where the glacier tumbled down to form the cwm. On the surrounding ledges and crevices, the base-rich soils allowed many species of arctic plants to flourish, including the rare Snowdon Lily. Rising from the east shores of the lake are the Idwal Slabs – great, diagonally angled crags of polished rock. With forbidding names such as the Suicide Wall, the crags have been attracting climbers for many decades.

To the east of Cwm Idwal lies Cwm Bochlwyd, a more airy hollow accommodating an equally large tarn. Although it's dominated by neighbours Tryfan and Glyder Fach, there's a fine ridge, Y Gribin (not to be confused with the one of the same name on Snowdon), which provides an exhilarating stairway to Glyder Fawr's summit plateau. Others, which include the Cneifion Arête and the Seniors' Ridge, require a greater degree of scrambling or climbing ability.

Glyder Fawr shows a gentler nature to Nant Gwryd in the south, its slopes comprising largely heather and craggy outcrops, but turn the corner into the Llanberis Pass and the mountain reverts to type, the crags of Esgair Felen forming a fierce face that shows no deference to Crib Goch or Snowdon.

Opposite: Typically spiky rocks on Glyder Fawr's summit plateau.
Right: On Yr Gribin looking to Tryfan and Llyn Bochlwyd.

Route G11
Y Gribin

A steep pull among spectacular scenery,
   finishing with a fine scramble

Start: Lay-by car park (GR: SH 656602)
Distance: 2 miles/3km
Height gain: 2330ft/710m
Time: 2 hours

Involves a Grade 1 scramble

Over the ladder stile at the back of the car park a pitched path climbs steeply up a rocky bank. The path soon becomes intermittent as it heads south-west across grassland towards the Bochlwyd stream, which it fords above a waterfall. It maintains direction to meet the paved Miners' Track, which it follows south-eastwards. Hereabouts, the views are dominated by Tryfan (left) and Y Garn (right). There's a steep paved section climbing to the

outflow of Llyn Bochlwyd, a shallow but size-able tarn shaded by the immense north slopes of Glyder Fach.

Most walkers will be continuing along the Miners' Track for Bwlch Tryfan here, but this route turns right along a less distinct path which heads for the base of the Gribin ridge. A path turns left and climbs up the spur, giving fine views of both Bochlwyd and Y Garn. Llyn Idwal is soon added to the scene.

After traversing a flat, grassy shelf in the middle of the spur, the route becomes more serious: a Grade 1 scramble over the rocky crest. It's easier than Crib Goch and, in good conditions, should present no problems to the fit and experienced walker. More often than not there's an easier route on the west side of the crest. Gribin ends just west of Bwlch y Ddwy Glyder. For Glyder Fawr just turn right along an easy cairned route.

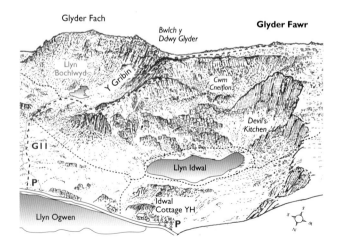

Route G12
Cwm Idwal and the Devil's Kitchen

*The most popular way and the most scenic
    . . . at first*

Start: Idwal Cottage car park
    (GR: SH 649603)
Distance: 2¼ miles/3.5km
Height gain: 2330ft/710m
Time: 2–2½ hours

This route first follows the crowds on the Cwm Idwal Nature Trail, which starts by the left side of the toilet block and climbs past some boisterous waterfalls to reach Llyn Idwal. Go around the left side of the lake, but leave the lakeside path to pass beneath the climbers on the Idwal Slabs. Beyond the stream, Nant Ifan, the path zigzags over rough boulders to the foot of the Devil's Kitchen, where an engineered path angles left up the rock face to arrive at the grassy hollow of Llyn Cwn. A bouldery gulley path climbs from the north-east of the small lake. Take care on this section, which can be loose and slippery, especially in wintry conditions. After a slithery grind you arrive on Glyder Fawr's rocky plateau.

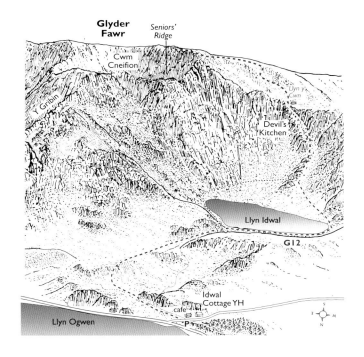

Route G13

Pen y Gwryd and Bwlch y Ddwy Glyder

*A rough route with few paths – for
masochists only*

Start: Llyn Lockwood, Pen y Gwryd
(GR: SH 662559)

Distance: 2¼ miles/3.5km

Height gain: 2400ft/730m

Time: 2 hours

As in Route G10 to Glyder Fach, the path begins at the roadside ladder opposite the car park and crosses the footbridge spanning Nant Gwryd. After going over the ladder stile in the fence beyond, leave the main path and head left across marshy ground to another ladder stile. Beyond this follow the stream north-westwards into Cwm Ffynnon. At the 379m spot height, climb northwards by the east bank of Llyn Cwmffynnon's main feeder stream. The marshy ground is soon replaced by trackless heather-and-rock slopes. Looking back you'll be able to see the squarish tarn in its marshy hollow.

Ahead, the ground rears up to the harsh bouldery south-eastern slopes of the Glyder ridge. The thick tussocky nature of the heather makes the going very hard indeed as the slopes of Glyder Fawr (left) and Glyder Fach (right) close in to form a passage. Ahead lies the pass of Bwlch y Ddwy Glyder, easily recognized by the spear-like rocks of Castell y Gwynt.

At the foot of the 'castle' the route finally meets a proper cairned path which climbs left up the easy stony ridge to Glyder Fawr's summit plateau.

Glyder Fawr

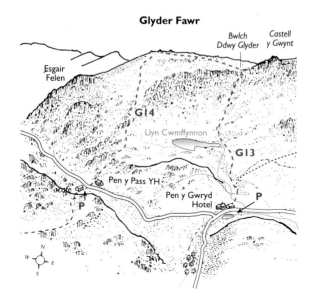

Route G14
Pen y Pass and Cwm Ffynnon

*The most direct southern approach, a fine
route with wonderful views of Crib Goch
and Yr Wyddfa*

Start: Pay car park at Pen y Pass
(GR: SH 647556)
Distance: 2 miles/3km
Height gain: 2100ft/640m
Time: 1½ hours

Note: Would be difficult in mist

The path begins from a gate at the west side
of the youth hostel and climbs among the
crags to a low grassy ridge overlooking Llyn
Cwmffynnon and its marshy hollow. Turn left
to climb the long grassy arm that forms a
vague extension of Glyder Fawr's broad south
ridge. After descending slightly to a marshy
area, the faint path climbs north-westwards
to rockier ground. Occasional splashes of
paint on the rocks mark the route, which
climbs steeply away from the complex cliffs
of the Llanberis Pass. The scene across the
pass to Crib Goch and Carnedd Ugain is
breathtaking, with views directly into Cwm
Glas and the famous climbers' crags of Dinas
Mot, Gyrn Las and Clogwyn y Person.

After weaving through rocky outcrops, the
path comes to Glyder Fawr's stony plateau,
where cairns lead to the summit.

Below: Descending Route G14 from Glyder Fawr with the Snowdon massif ahead.

Route G15
Nant Peris and Cwm Padrig

Though steep, one of the prettiest routes and on the quiet side of the mountain

Start: Park and ride car park at Nant Peris (GR: SH 606584)

Distance: 3 miles/5km including walk up the road

Height gain: 2950ft/900m

Time: 2–2½ hours

Turn right out of the park-and-ride car park and follow the road in the direction of the Llanberis Pass. After passing through the hamlet of Gwastadnant and crossing the Afon Las, leave the road for a signed footpath which uses a farm drive lined by slate walls.

At the end of the drive, go over a ladder stile lying just to the left of a stone cottage. The path, indistinct for a short way, climbs slightly left up sheep-mown grassy slopes interspersed with boulders. It nears the bounding stream of Afon Las to reach another ladder stile. Across this the path becomes stony and meanders up steep grassy slopes, dominated by rocky bluffs and the deciduous woods that line the stream.

A metal footbridge allows the crossing of a side stream and the path continues steeply uphill, rounding the right side of an impressive bluff, then skirting left of another.

The scenery gets wilder but less beautiful as height is gained. The boulder path meets and joins a streamside fence before crossing

Glyder Fawr

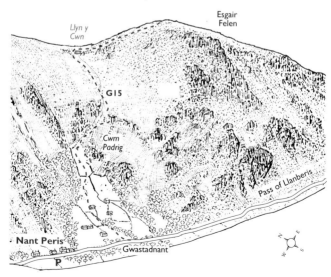

it at a ladder stile. The Afon Las has divided just below. Ford the near stream, then follow a faint path alongside the far stream.

The path soon strikes out on its own to reach Llyn y Cwn, a small tarn set beneath the grassy slopes of Y Garn and the loose and shaley west flank of Glyder Fawr. After rounding the tarn on the left, a path up a bouldery gulley starts up Glyder Fawr's loose western slopes. (Note: In descent the route is rather unpleasant and can become dangerous in wintry conditions.) After a slithery slog up the shaley slopes, the path attains Glyder Fawr's rocky plateau.

Note on descent: two-thirds of the way down Cwm Padraig, it's easy to miss the path and find yourself looking over a large crag. A few paces back, the path has turned left to round this crag on the east side.

Other route options

Competent scramblers could divert from the lower regions of the Y Cribin ridge (Route G11) into Cwm Cneifion before tackling the Seniors' Ridge.

RIDGE ROUTES

Glyder Fach

Distance: 1 mile/1.5km
Height gain: 245ft/75m
Time: ¼ hour

Follow a line of cairns across Glyder Fawr's bouldery plateau, descending gradually to Bwlch y Ddwy Glyder, a pass looking down on Y Gribin's cliffs to Llyn Bochlwyd.

The way ahead is blocked by the spiky rock towers of Castell y Gwynt. A path descends to the right of the castle before clambering over the boulder slopes back to the ridge beyond it. Although you'll lose more height this way, it's much easier. The path continues across stony ground to the pile of boulders marking Glyder Fach's summit.

Y Garn

Distance: 1¼ miles/ 2km
Height gain: 820ft/250m
Time: ¾–1 hour

Follow the cairned path to the eastern edge of the plateau before descending on an unpleasantly loose, winding path down to Llyn y Cwn. After going around the right side of the shallow tarn, a well-worn path climbs up Y Garn's grassy slopes. It soon divides, and either fork will do. The right goes closer to the edge of Cwm Clyd, the left leads more directly to the summit.

Anyone who's been to Ogwen and stood beside its lake will remember the mountain that soars into the skies from the head of Nant Ffrancon. Although it's watched over by Tryfan, Pen yr Ole Wen and Glyder Fawr, Ogwen is totally dominated by Y Garn, which has the awe-inspiring presence of an Everest, an Eiger or a Jungfrau.

Y Garn, which simply means the cairn, has two ridges which enclose the hanging valley of Cwm Clyd. The shorter, steeper East Ridge is serious stuff for the walker and best left to climbers or serious scramblers – it is generally classified as a Grade 2 scramble. The North-east ridge, although steep and loose in places, offers good routes to the top with inti-mate views of Cwm Clyd, an idyllic hollow with two lakes: one a small circular pool, the other a larger tarn with an isthmus of crag that gives it the shape of a crumbling molar tooth when seen from above. Cwm Clyd is a wonderful place to come for a picnic, and can be accessed either from the South-east Ridge path or the narrow Fisherman's Path, which follows a stony course above the south bank of the outlet stream.

Cwm Cywion, the other side of the North-east Ridge, is a lonely place with two tiny pools set in a peaty hollow beneath tumbling scree slopes and sun-shy, craggy outcrops.

In the east, Y Garn shows a different face to the world. Here, a stone-scattered grass slope slips down towards Nant Peris. Even here there's one last stand, with the mighty crag of Dinas watching over the village.

Opposite: Cwm Idwal from the low slopes of Y Garn.
Below: Y Garn, Llyn Idwal and Nant Ffrancon Valley from Glyder Fawr.

Route G16
Cwm Idwal and the Devil's Kitchen

A classic mountain route
Start: Idwal Cottage YH (GR: SH 649603)
Distance: 2½ miles/3.5km
Height gain: 2130ft/650m
Time: 1½ hours

This route follows the Cwm Idwal Nature Trail, which starts by the left side of the toilet block. A wide track climbs gradually past some boisterous waterfalls before swinging right across open grassland. A fairly level path soon arrives by the shores of Llyn Idwal. There are useable routes on both sides of the lake but we will use the one around the east side. This stays fairly close to the lake shore before being abandoned for a path on the left which passes beneath the Idwal Slabs, where you'll almost certainly see climbers grappling with the smooth rock. Beyond the Nant Ifan stream, the path zigzags over rough boulders to the foot of the dark cliffs and the defile of the Devil's Kitchen.

Here an engineered path angles left up the rock face to arrive at the grassy hollow of Llyn Cwn, where the gravelly slopes of Glyder Fawr to the left face the more gentle grass slopes of Y Garn. Turn right along a well-used path climbing those grassy slopes. Use either the right fork edge path or the left fork to reach Y Garn's summit.

Opposite: Pen yr Ole Wen and Llyn Idwal from the Route G16 path up Devil's Kitchen.

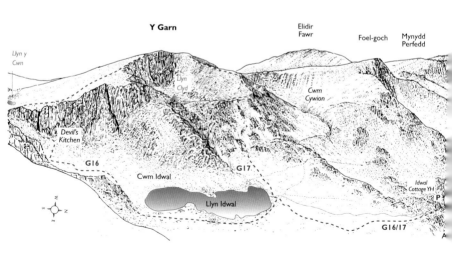

Above: Y Garn's crags above Idwal.

Route G17
Cwm Idwal and Y Garn's North-east Ridge
Steep but rewarding path
Start: Idwal Cottage YH (GR: SH 649603)
Distance: 5 miles/8km
Height gain: 3050ft/930m
Time: 3–3½ hours

As in Route G16, follow the Llyn Idwal Nature Trail from the left side of the toilet block to the lake. This time turn right over the footbridge across the outflow stream and trace the northern lake shore. Leave the main path to strike off along a westbound path heading for the base of Y Garn's North-east Ridge. The views back into Idwal and its great climbing slabs are tremendous, especially after rain when great white spout-like waterfalls come tumbling down the rock walls.

The path climbs the North-east Ridge, veering left into the lower regions of Cwm Clyd before curving right, back to the crest. The middle section is very steep and the zigzag path has been eroded by walkers' shortcuts. In the upper regions the ridge narrows, with precipitous drops into Cwm Clyd and Cwm Cywion. On reaching a cairn on the main Glyder ridge, turn left to climb to Y Garn's summit.

Route G18
Nant Peris and Cwm Padrig

An unrelentingly stiff climb to the ridge

Start: Nant Peris (GR: SH 607583)
Distance: 3 miles/5km
Height gain: 2760ft/840m
Time: 2 hours

Turn right out of the park-and-ride car park and follow the road towards the Llanberis Pass. Just beyond the hamlet of Gwastadnant, leave the road for a signed footpath on the left down a farm drive. At the end of the drive go over a ladder stile to the left of a cottage, then climb across a field towards the Afon Las stream. A stony path now meanders up steep grassy slopes, past crags and woodland which line the stream, then on to the higher, wilder terrain of Cwm Padrig, which lies between the rugged cliffs of Esgair Felen and the grassy pyramid of Y Garn. Go over a ladder stile in the fence, ford the first of two streams, then follow a faint path alongside the banks of the far stream. The path soon strikes out on its own to reach Llyn y Cwn, where you turn left to follow Route G16 up a wide, grassy ridge to the summit.

For the descent route, see the note on Route G15 (Glyder Fawr).

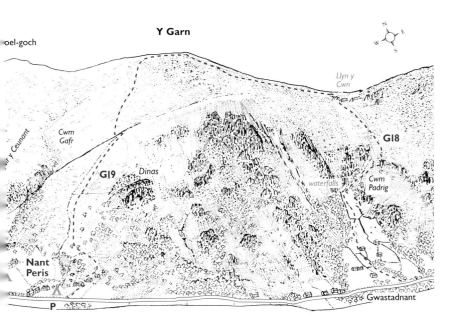

Route G19
Nant Peris and Cwm Gafr

A tough slog up but good for descent
Start: Nant Peris park-and-ride car park
  (GR: SH 607583)
Distance: 2¼ miles/3.5 km
Height gain: 2760ft/840m
Time: 1½ hours

A path from behind the car park's toilets leads back to the village's main road, opposite the terraced houses and green of Nant Ffynnon. Turn right then left along the lane bordering the green. This passes the Cae Gwyn campsite before entering a courtyard between several buildings. Go through the gate opposite an old telephone kiosk and to the right of a stone barn. Here a gritty track leads half-right towards a small whitewashed cottage. A primitive slate bridge crosses a stream.

Keep as close to the cottage as possible to avoid the worst of a particularly marshy area just beyond the stream, then aim for some ruins beneath a tall sycamore tree. A path now climbs north-east, guided by a fence on the left and ladder stiles in the cross-fences. The craggy, castle-like knoll of Dinas is prominent in views to the right, which also show off Crib Goch and Carnedd Ugain's climbing grounds to perfection.

The path now comes to the open country of Cwm Gafr beyond a ladder stile (GR 616 592). Eventually it fords the side stream and continues north-eastwards up the grassy cwm.

A faint path from Cwm Ceunant comes in from the left and should be followed up the west flanks of Y Garn. The route reaches the ridge north of Y Garn's summit. You find yourself looking over the lonely Cwm Cywion and its tiny twin pools. (Note: If you missed the path in fog, a fence coming in diagonally from the Ceunant ridge on the left will guide you to the ridge.)

Turn right to climb the ridge – you'll soon be joined by the popular path from Ogwen – to reach the summit.

Descent
Finding the path doesn't matter too much at the beginning of this route, because the terrain is quite good. The easiest way is to head northwards to the point where the North-east Ridge meets the main ridge before descending south-westwards into Cwm Gafr. Lower down the mountainside, streams on the left will guide you down to the ladder stile on the edge of open country. (Make sure you don't get too low – that is close to the Afon Gafr – or you'll miss the ladder stile.)

Continue south-west aiming for the ladder stiles in intervening walls to reach a small whitewashed cottage. Go to the right side of this and use a slate plank bridge to cross a streamlet and gain access to a track that comes to the courtyard of the Cae Gwyn campsite and bunkhouse. Follow the tarred lane along the left side of the camping field out to the main road.

Other route options

It is possible, although it's tough, to follow Route G20 (Foel-goch) into Cwm Cywion and climb out of the cwm to Bwlch y Cywion on the ridge to the north of Y Garn's summit. Although I've never tried it, the passage from Cwm Cywion to Y Garn's North-east Ridge looks loose and unappealing as it nears the crest.

RIDGE ROUTES

Glyder Fawr

Distance: 1¼ miles/ 2km
Height gain: 985ft/300m
Time: ¼–1 hour

Descend SSE along the stony rim of Cwm Clyd before heading down grass slopes towards Llyn y Cwn, a small tarn set in a grassy upland hollow above the Devil's Kitchen. Go around the left side of the tarn and climb on a loose path up a bouldery gulley beyond its north-east shores. Take care on this section, which can be loose and slippery, especially in wintry conditions. Eventually the path deposits you on the easier ground of Glyder Fawr's stony summit plateau.

Foel-goch

Distance: 1¼ miles/2km
Height gain: 260ft/80m
Time: ¼–1 hour

This straightforward route descends around the rim of Cwm Cywion. Ignore the well-used left fork, which bypasses Foel-goch altogether, but instead stay with the ridge, climbing over a small grassy knoll before going down a small dip to Bwlch y Cywion. From here, there's a short climb on grass to Foel-goch's summit. You may wish to make a short diversion to the right from the pass along the Llymllwyd ridge. This offers views across to Foel-goch's tremendous cliffs and to those of Creigiau Gleision and the Mushroom Garden.

Overleaf: Foel-goch, Y Garn and Glyder Fawr soar above the verdant Nant Peris, with the seemingly tiny houses of Gwastadnant dwarfed by the crags of Ysgair Felen on the right.

The fact that Foel-goch, the red hill, isn't a 3000-footer means it doesn't get the respect it deserves. This is a fine mountain with some of the best crags in the whole of the Glyderau. The summit is pyramidal with two magnificent rock ridges descending into Nant Ffrancon.

Early travellers would have by-passed Foel-goch using the ancient packhorse route over Bwlch y Brecan. Many would have found the almost sunless crag face of Foel-goch's notched north-east ridge, Y Esgair, rather daunting, and would have been in a hurry to get down to Nant Ffrancon and Bangor. Also by-passing Foel-goch are the runners and fast walkers who are doing the Welsh 3000s. As it's of no interest to them, they use a little path round the back in a mad dash to get to Y Garn without too much effort.

Competent scramblers and climbers can often be seen on Creigiau Gleision's Mushroom Garden (Grade 2). In his book *Scrambles and Easy Climbs in Snowdonia* Jon Sparks poetically described the scene: 'Creigiau Gleision . . . sprawls across the north-east flank like an opium smoker on a divan.' The ridge-top here offers the walker a great way to the top and can be tackled from Cwm Cywion by way of a shoulder, luxuriantly cloaked with heather, grass and bilberry. On the other side of Cwm Coch, so called because of the red screes that tumble from the foot of the crags, is Yr Esgair, the shorter and more serious ridge.

Although, like Y Garn, Foel-goch suffers the indignity of a soft grass underbelly on the Nant Peris side, it does have one magnificent route – the narrow Esgair y Ceunant ridge – where there's a short craggy section followed by an easy walk across wide flanks of pallid, wind-ruffled moor grass.

The bottom line is that Foel-goch is part of a superb grass ridgewalk taking in all the mountains from Y Garn to Carnedd y Filiast – or even Elidir Fach – and you just cannot beat it for panoramic views.

Opposite: Foel-goch from Llyn Ogwen.
Right: Foel-goch and Bwlch y Brecan.

Route G20
Nant Ffrancon and Cwm Cywion

A tough (in the early stages) but rewarding route

Start: Car park by Idwal Cottage YH
(GR: SH 649603)
Distance: 2 miles/ 3km
Height gain: 1870ft/570m
Time: 1½ hours

Note: The car park fills up rapidly. There are others by the shores of Llyn Ogwen

---

From the car park in front of the Idwal Cottage Youth Hostel, turn right along the minor lane through the trees, descending into the Nant Ffrancon valley to pass Yr Hafod hostel.

Just beyond the hostel, a short vehicle track on the left marks the best place to begin the slog up the grass slopes beneath Cwm Cywion. The track soon fades, but climb west to the ladder stile in the fence. An intermittent path begins again, keeping south of Cywion's outlet stream. On approaching a stone cross-wall head for the second opening from the left of the stream.

The path, now more prominent, continues in an easier fashion. Keep watch for a zigzag scree path on slopes to the right. The bottom of this marks the point where you need to ford the stream. The scree path gains height quickly and soon becomes a pleasant path weaving its way over grass slopes which are interspersed with rock outcrops and beds of

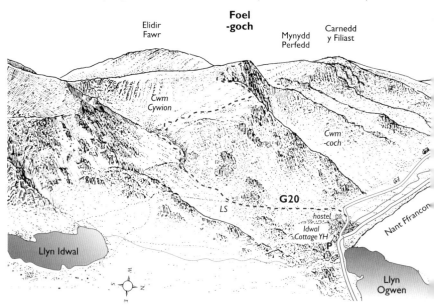

Above: On the ridge above the Mushroom Gardens, with Tryfan, Glyder Fach and Glyder Fawr in the distance.

bilberry. Looking south, there's a splendid view across Cwn Cywion and its two tiny tarns to Y Garn. Although there's as much scree as crag on its slopes, Y Garn still boasts graceful, flowing slopes upon which, if you're lucky, the sunlight will play.

Things get more exciting as the path meets the crags at the top of the Mushroom Gardens. Between the impressive crags are precipitous scree gulleys. Beyond the Mushroom Gardens, an airy edge path turns left on to Y Llymllwyd, Foel-goch's south-east ridge. The scenes are typical of the Glyderau, with dark glaciated cliffs plummeting to a tight rocky cwm known as Cwm Coch. Rather than make a bee-line for Foel-goch across its eroded southern slopes, the path maintains its westerly direction to meet the main Glyder ridge just north of Bwlch Cywion. Here a fence guides the path easily to the summit.

Route G21

Nant Peris and Esgair y Ceunant

A splendid, little-used route

Start: Nant Peris park-and-ride car park
  (GR: SH 607583)

Distance: 2¼ miles/4.5 km

Height gain: 2390ft/730m

Time: 2 hours

On returning to the main road, turn left, passing the Vaynol Arms before turning right on the lane by the old chapel. Follow this as it turns left past the Ty-isaf campsite entrance.

Just beyond the whitewashed Nant yr Fron cottage (not the Fron marked on the map – that's a couple of hundred metres further along the lane), go through a gate and continue along the lane. A gate on the right high-

lighted by a footpath sign marks the start of the path on to the mountain. Strike uphill to a stile by another gate. The clear path enters access land beyond another ladder stile and a zigzag grass track climbs into the valley of the Afon Dudodyn. On the far bank, slate from the Llanberis quarries is piled high but the eyes will be on Elidir Fawr, which rises above these industrial indignities.

The track comes to a footbridge across the Dudodyn (GR 608596), but stay with the track which continues alongside the south bank. After going through the next gate, leave it for a worn grass path heading for Esgair y Ceunant, the rock-interspersed ridge ahead. A stone wall guides the route up and along the ridge, which becomes increasingly rocky. Beyond a ladder stile and a very useful (if it's

Foel-goch

196

raining) sheepfold, the wall becomes a fence. The view ahead is one of smooth-profiled grassy moors surrounding the high pass of Bwlch y Brecan.

The fence veers half-right away from the ridge and across the moors to the pass between Y Garn and Foel-goch, but stay with the ridge until a right fork path leads the route to the main Glyder ridge south of Foel-goch. Turn left here. The path is guided by a ridge fence leading to Foel-goch's summit.

Note: Towards the end of Esgair y Ceunant a good path arcs to Bwlch y Brecan where you can tackle Foel-goch. However, the main ridge path here zigzags up horribly loose and eroded scree.

Other route options

There's a steep, pathless route climbing the open hillside to the south of Maes Caradoc into Cwm Bual. By keeping north of the stream, well away from the gorge, the route can join a path climbing right to the crest of a spur between Cwm Bual and Cwm Perfedd. By keeping to the south side, you can climb left to a ladder stile which gives access to a stony path that traces the foot of Yr Esgair, Foel-goch's North-east Ridge. At the next ladder stile turn right and gain the previously mentioned spur higher up the crest. Both routes climb to the ridge at Bwlch y Brecan north of Foel-goch.

Below: Esgair y Ceunant ridge above Nant Peris.

RIDGE ROUTES

Y Garn

Distance: 1¼ miles/2km
Height gain: 655ft/200m
Time: ¼–1 hour

A fence leads the route south along the grassy ridge down to Bwlch y Cywion. After going over a grassy knoll and down to another unnamed pass, the route begins the climb around the rim of Cwm Cywion towards Y Garn. The ground becomes increasingly stony as the north-east ridge path comes in from the left at a cairn, and the route winds up to the summit.

Mynydd Perfedd

Distance: 2–3 miles/1km
Height gain: 260ft/80m
Time: ½ hour

The path to Bwlch y Brecan zigzags down reddish screes and becomes increasingly loose. The difficulties are short-lived, however, as the pass is grassy and the path good. The direct path to Mynydd Perfedd leaves the main Elidir Fawr path to follow a ridge fence steeply uphill to Mynydd Perfedd's south rim. Here the fence turns left and ceases to be of any use. Maintain the north-westerly course over a stone-and-grass plateau to the cairned summit.

Below: Above Foel-goch's Creigiau Gleision rocks with the summit ahead.
Opposite: Foel-goch and Nant Peris showing Esgair Ceunant ridge.

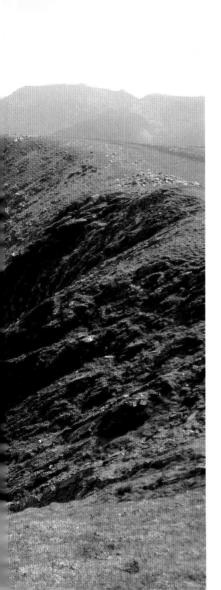

MYNYDD PERFEDD

The name Mynydd Perfedd, which means central mountain (or intestine mountain, if you look it up in a really comprehensive Welsh dictionary), is rather grand for such an insignificant summit. If the mountain were not over 2000ft and on the main Glyder ridge, it probably wouldn't receive many visitors, and those who do come would quickly move on.

Mynydd Perfedd's western flanks have been spoiled by the building of the Marchlyn Mawr dam. The desolate reservoir waters often go down the plug-hole when the people of Llanberis need electricity, leaving a sterile, stony tidemark exposed.

Mynydd Perfedd is also upstaged by the craggy cone of Foel-goch and the great massif of Elidir Fawr, but the mountain does have its moments. Wander by the fence to the rock outcrops on the west rim. Here is a wonderful vantage point for Elidir Fawr, which appears like a pyramid, fragmented by shady cliffs and screes. Looking up at Mynydd Perfedd from Nant Ffrancon shows that the mountain possesses an impressive spur, with steep flowing slopes etched on both sides by scree and accentuated by squat cliffs and spiky outcrops.

Opposite: Mynydd Perfedd's face above Cwm Graianog.

Route G22
Nant Ffrancon

A rather devious but fascinating panoramic route below climbing grounds

Start: Idwal Cottage YH (GR: SH 649603)
Distance: 2 ¼ miles/4.5km
Height gain: 1870ft/570m
Time: 1 ½ hours

Note: The car park fills up rapidly but there are others by the shores of Llyn Ogwen

---

From the car park in front of the Idwal Cottage Youth Hostel, turn right along the minor lane through the trees, descending into the valley of Nant Ffrancon. After passing Yr Hafod hostel, a short vehicle track on the left marks the best place to begin the slog up the grass slopes beneath Cwm Cywion. The track soon fades, but climb west to a ladder stile in the fence. An intermittent path keeps south of Cywion's outlet stream.

On the approach to the upper cwm, angle right for the point where a prominent dry-stone wall meets the stream (GR 637604). Ford the stream (which is rarely difficult) and angle slightly uphill for a few paces. This will bring you to a delightful narrow path, which

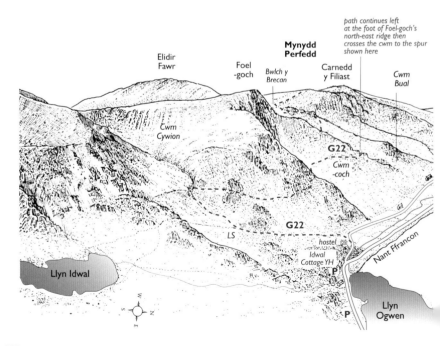

leads the route north beneath the crags of the Mushroom Gardens into Cwm-coch, where Creigiau Gleision's rocks tower above. The little path edges around Foel-goch's North-east Ridge into Cwm Bual, where it turns left by a wall.

Well into the cwm turn right over a ladder stile (GR 629614) and head north on a track-less course to the grassy ridge that divides Cwm Bual and Cwm Perfedd. On reaching the crest, climb left to locate a stony path, the remains of an old packhorse route between Nant Peris and Nant Ffrancon. This meanders up to Bwlch y Brecan.

After going over a ladder stile at the pass, turn right to follow the ridge fence on to Mynydd Perfedd. This requires that you leave the main path, which curves left towards Elidir Fawr. Mynydd Perfedd's summit shelter lies on a stone-and-grass plateau beyond another ladder stile.

Below: The fine ledge path around Foel-goch.

Route G23

Nant Peris and Cwm Dudodyn

A rather dull route

Start: Nant Peris park-and-ride car park
   (GR: SH 607583)

Distance: 3 miles/5km

Height gain: 2300ft/700m

Time: 2 hours

Turn left along the main road, passing the Vaynol Arms before turning right on the lane by the old chapel. Follow this as it turns left past the Ty-isaf camp site entrance and the whitewashed Nant yr Fron cottage. Before reaching the last house and the end of the lane, go through a gate on the right highlighted by a footpath sign and strike uphill to a stile and gate at the top of a field. The clear path enters access land beyond another ladder stile and a zigzagging grass track climbs into the valley of the Afon Dudodyn, where the slate from the Llanberis quarries is piled high. Ignore the footbridge across the Dudodyn (GR 608596), but stay with the track as it continues alongside the stream's south-east bank.

Where all signs of a path give up, follow the stream to the head of the cwm before

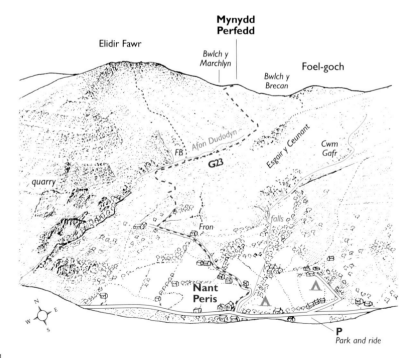

tackling the steep grassy slopes on the left to Bwlch y Marchlyn, where you look down fine cliffs to the reservoir. Climb right on a path by a fence to Mynydd Mawr's grassy summit plateau. Go over a ladder stile in the fence to continue to the summit cairn.

Other route options

There are no perfect beeline routes to Mynydd Perfedd; its upper slopes are too steep and unstable for that. It is possible to ascend the steep grass slopes either side of the fields of Maes Caradoc farm before climbing into Cwm Perfedd. The route would then continue to Bwlch y Brecan by way of the grassy spur dividing Cwm Perfedd and Cwm Bual. The narrow ridge of Esgair y Ceunant (see Route G21) would also offer a direct ascent. A clear path from near the end of the ridge arcs left around the rim of Cwm Dudodyn to Bwlch y Brecan and onwards to Bwlch y Marchlyn. At this pass double back right (north-east) to the summit of Mynydd Perfedd.

A direct ascent from Cwm Marchlyn would be halted by a tall stone wall climbing from near the reservoir dam. It has no stiles until you reach the crest of the Carnedd y Filiast ridge.

RIDGE ROUTES

Foel-goch

Distance: 2–3 miles/1km
Height gain: 400ft/120m
Time: ½ hour

A simple route following the ridge fence down grassy slopes to Bwlch y Brecan. The climb isn't as pleasant and consists of a winding path up loose red scree slopes. An alternative path around the eastern side of Foel-goch goes to Bwlch y Cywion, where a grassy ridge path doubles back left to the summit.

Elidir Fawr

Distance: 1 mile/1.5km
Height gain: 690ft/210m
Time: ¼ hour

Descend along the rim of Cwm Marchlyn and up a narrow rocky arête. The path and ridge get wider in the mid-stages before the path continues its climb over the bouldery terrain of the summit.

Carnedd y Filiast

Distance: 2–3 miles/1km
Height gain: 985ft/30m
Time: ½ hour

A very easy stroll across a grassy ridge with stony patches. On reaching the bouldery dome of Carnedd y Filiast, keep right for easier ground before climbing left for the wind shelter.

CARNEDD Y FILIAST

Carnedd y Filiast is the most northerly of the Glyderau peaks lining the glacial U-shaped valley of Nant Ffrancon. Its name means cairn of the greyhound bitch – a strange name for a hill which, it has been suggested, has connections with Ceridwen, the Celtic goddess of nature, poetry and all things mystical. It is said the lady, who also had a dark side, turned herself into a greyhound to pursue her foe, Gwion, who had turned himself into a hare in order to escape.

You cannot escape the fact that Carnedd y Filiast has been disfigured by the Penrhyn quarrymen, who have over the centuries been responsible for devastating excavations into the north side of the mountain. Still, these northern Glyderau ridges are a joy: grassy promenades where you can stroll to distant horizons with little effort.

Carnedd y Filiast's summit is a jumble of large grey boulders, rising to the wind shelter on the top. To the west scree-grazed bilberry slopes fall in graceful arcs to the rather sulky, unkempt Cwm Marchlyn, a place of rushes and thistles, and where the upper valley has been dammed to form a large reservoir that supplies the Dinorwic Hydroelectric Power Station with its head of water.

Opposite: The Atlantic Slabs on Carnedd y Filiast.

Two ridges flank the hanging valleys of Cwm Ceunant and Cwm Graianog. The north-east ridge is smoother, cloaked with bilberry and heather, while the east ridge, which divides the two cwms, is bereft of any vegetation. Here smooth, almost white slabs, the largest being the Atlantic Slabs, come to the surface. Although easily angled, these expansive and spectacular sandstone crags have few handholds and pose some difficult questions for climbers, but offer merely solace to the eye of the humble walker.

Route G24

Ogwen Bank and Ffronllwyd

A fine, seldom-trodden route

Start: Ogwen Bank (GR: SH 627654)

Distance: 3 miles/5km

Height gain: 2000ft/610m

Time: 2 hours

From the road bridge at Ogwen Bank, head down the tarred quarry road bordering the river. Turn left through a wooden gate on to a wide, stony track which passes beneath the spoil heaps of the Penrhyn quarry. The undulating track is also used as a cycle track, so keep to one side to allow cyclists to pass.

The spoil heaps are slowly being vegetated and trees and bushes are taking hold. Beyond the caravan site, which can be seen through the trees on the Ogwen's far banks, the river

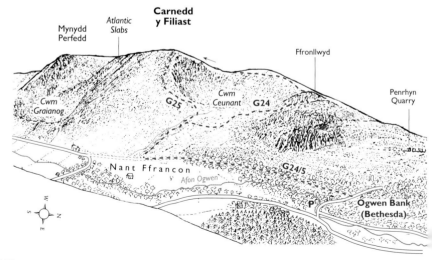

breaks free into the verdant pastures of Nant Ffrancon, with the long grassy ridge of Braich Ty Du leading the eye gently towards Pen yr Ole Wen and Carnedd Dafydd.

Leave the track at a gate (GR 629639) for a faint path which almost immediately crosses a streamlet then climbs firm grass slopes towards a patch of scree by the main Ceunant stream.

On reaching the scree, the path climbs up a spur of rock, heather and bilberry on the north bank of the Ceunant. Ignore the path which drops down to the stream but look out for a narrow path breaking right by a large tree (GR 625637). The path soon becomes more prominent and climbs steadily across more slopes, still thick with bilberry and heather. The course of this path is more winding than the straight one marked on the OS map with black dashes. It turns left steeply up a grassy patch before veering right towards the crags of Ffronllwyd, Carnedd y Filiast's north-eastern spur. A small cairn marks the start of the ridge path, which soon comes to a large crag. Scramble up the diagonal slabs to gain the heather-and-rock ridge, which climbs to a subsidiary peak at spot height 721m.

After rounding the rim of Cwm Ceunant, follow a loose, stony path that climbs towards the summit of Carnedd y Filiast. The last 50m is a clamber over the huge boulders covering the summit. Among the boulders a large wind shelter provides a good lunch stop.

Below: The North-west Ridge of Carnedd y Filiast.

Route G25
Ogwen Bank and the East Ridge

A tough route in the early stages, but
*   rewarding*
Start: Ogwen Bank (GR: SH 627654)
Distance: 3 miles/5km
Height gain: 2000ft/610m
Time: 2 hours

Follow Route G24 from Ogwen Bank into Nant Ffrancon and again go through the gate at GR 629639. Aim for the clearly visible streamside scree patch and follow the spur on the north bank of the Ceunant. On this route continue higher into Cwm Ceunant before breaking left on an intermittent path heading for the east ridge. A path develops on a fairly steep climb above the cwm. It becomes prominent and stony in the upper reaches and takes the route straight up to the summit boulders.

Below: Near the top of Carnedd y Filiast's East Ridge

Route G26
Cwm Marchlyn and Carnedd y Filiast
Another tough but rewarding route
Start: Deiniolen (GR: SH 59663)
Distance: 2¼ miles/3.5km
Height gain: 2490ft/760m
Time: 1½ hours

Go through the gate at the end of the public road and follow the roadside path past the crater of an old quarry. Ignore the right fork track beyond this but where your track swings right on the first part of a zigzag, leave it to maintain direction across a thistle and rush-strewn field. This short-cut brings the route back to the road, which eases beneath Marchlyn Mawr's dam (note how the builders have added scree to make the grassy dam look like a natural hillside). A path descends left from the roadside to cross the dry outlet of the reservoir from where it recrosses the track and climbs to a ladder stile (GR 617 625).

A good path now rakes up heather-and-grass slopes to a grassy saddle just below the unnamed top (721m spot height). After looking over the western edge into Cwm Ceunant, climb right on an increasingly stony path towards Carnedd y Filiast. The last 50m is a clamber over the huge boulders crowning the summit.

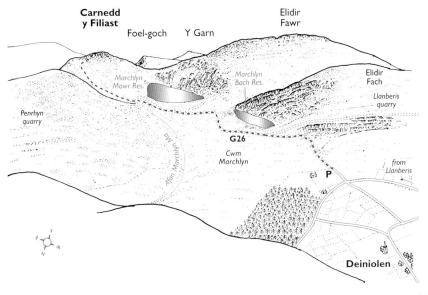

Other route options

None, unless you're a climber who is competent to tackle the great slabs of Cwm Graianog. These are highly dangerous to the uninitiated.

RIDGE ROUTES

Mynydd Perfedd

Distance: 2–3 miles/1km
Height gain: 65ft/20m
Time: ½ hour

After clambering down from the wind shelter on Carnedd y Filiast's summit, the path becomes easier, a pleasant stroll in fact, across a wide, stone-strewn grass ridge. After going over a ladder stile in a cross-wall the path comes close to the Atlantic Slabs. It's worthwhile staying with the western edge from here because you get splendid views of the great rock faces facing Nant Ffrancon. The spur on the south side of Cwm Graianog gives unrivalled views back to the Atlantic Slabs. The path from here eases to Mynydd Perfedd's rounded summit where there is a cairn, but little else, except the route to Elidir Fawr, which has been beckoning for a while.

Below: Mynydd Perfedd (left) and Carnedd y Filiast (right), seen from Nant Ffrancon.

Above: Elidir Fawr and Elidir Fach across Marchlyn Bach Reservoir.

The real name for this 3000ft northern outlier of the Glyder range is Carn Elidir. Elidir was a great warrior and the son-in-law of Maelgwm, a bygone Prince of Gwynedd. When Maelgwm died leaving only an illegitimate son Rhun, Elidir, who had been the Prince's commander-in-chief, laid claim to the title. But Elidir was English and that didn't go down well with the locals who, it has to be said, preferred bastards to Englishmen. Elidir lost the battle and this summit was his consolation prize.

But Elidir's mountain has lost some battles too. The quarryman's axe and gunpowder have blown its sides into oblivion and its beautiful tarn, Llyn Marchlyn Mawr, has been cased in concrete in the name of cheap off-peak electricity. Seen from Llanberis, Elidir Fawr is a mess, with terrace upon terrace of purple-grey slate piled high like a great scab that won't heal. Elidir's pale grassy west face peeps sheepishly down on the scene.

When viewed from Cwm Dudodyn in the south, the mountain shows barren stony sides leading up to a crinkled crest – a scene that's imposing in magnitude but possessing nothing to capture the imagination. But view Elidir Fawr from Carnedd Dafydd or Pen yr Ole Wen and you see a different side to its nature. Now it rises above Nant Ffrancon, Foel-goch and Mynydd Perfedd as a proud pointed peak boasting gnarled crag faces and flowing screes. Maybe the big Elidir *is* worth a visit after all.

Route G27 Nant Peris

The Welsh 3000s route to the top
Start: Nant Peris park-and-ride car park
   (GR: SH 607583)
Distance: 2¼ miles/4.5 km
Height gain: 2390ft/730m
Time: 2 hours

On returning to the main road from the car park turn left, passing the Vaynol Arms before turning right on the lane by the old chapel. Follow this as swings left past the Ty-isaf campsite entrance and the whitewashed Nant yr Fron cottage. Just before the last house turn right through a gate on a signed footpath which strikes uphill to a stile by another gate. Beyond another ladder stile a zigzag grass path climbs into the valley of the Afon Dudodyn. On the far banks the slate from the Llanberis quarries is piled high, but the eyes will be on Elidir Fawr, which rises high above the slate heaps.

Cross the footbridge spanning the Afon Dudodyn (GR 608596), a splendid tree-lined stream bounding over its rocky bed in small waterfalls and whitewater torrents. The narrow path is now relentless in its pursuit of the top, and rakes up a vague spur before traversing Elidir Fawr's south flanks. High up the mountainside grass turns to boulders and the path makes the ridge close to the summit wind shelters.

Opposite: Retrospective view down Route G27.
Overleaf: Elidir Fawr (right) seen from across Nant Peris.

Elidir Fawr

2. THE GLYDERAU

Route G28
Cwm Marchlyn and Elidir Fach

A fine mountain walk once you've achieved Elidir Fach's northern spur

Start: Deiniolen (GR: SH 596631)
Distance: 4¼ miles/7km
Height gain: 2590ft/790m
Time: 2½ hours

From the road-end a tarred reservoir road heads for the hills, passing left of the old Llanberis Quarry and some very bleak high moor farmland which looks as if it belongs in a Brontë novel.

At a junction of tracks close to the dam of Marchlyn Bach Reservoir, take the right fork, then turn almost immediately left. Climb over the next gate (padlocked to stop vehicular access) then climb right on a faint path, which stays close to the wall for a short way before veering left to climb Elidir Fach's northern spur.

The path dies out as it nears the plateau, but watch out for the loose stony path that rakes left up Elidir Fawr's scree-strewn face. This arrives on the bouldery crest a short way west of the summit shelter.

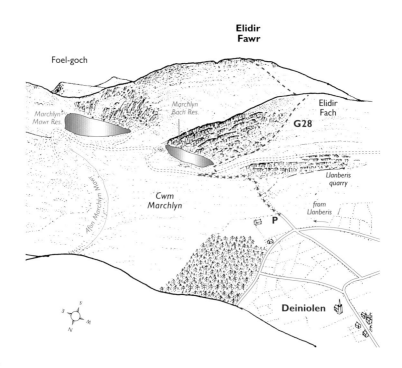

218

Other route options

A route does exist from the Marchlyn Mawr dam. It winds up a steep and loose scree slope before climbing the boulder slopes of the summit. The route is direct but the walker is subjected to a dismal, industrialized landscape on the way. The Afon Dudodoyn can be traced on a long and dull grassy trek to the head of the cwm. Then there's nowhere to go but up – climb left up very steep grassy slopes to Bwlch Marchlyn, where Elidir Fawr's eastern ridge leads the route to the summit.

RIDGE ROUTE

Mynydd Perfedd
Distance: 1 mile/1.5km
Height gain: 660ft/200m
Time: 1 hour

After boulder-hopping on the summit descend on an easier grass ridge that narrows to a rocky arête. Beyond Bwlch Marchlyn leave the main path (which is heading for Bwlch y Brecan) for one that climbs the grassy ridge to Mynydd Perfedd.

Below: Elidir Fawr rises like a pyramid from the shores of Marchlyn Mawr Reservoir.

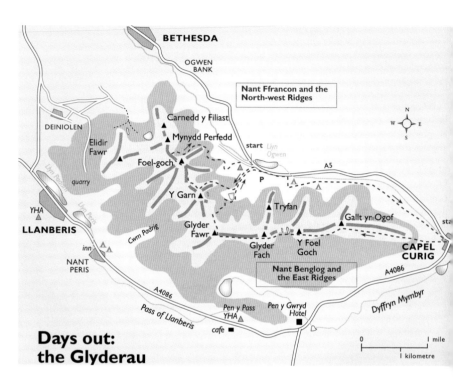

BETHESDA

OGWEN BANK

Nant Ffrancon and the North-west Ridges

N
W E
S

DEINIOLEN

Carnedd y Filiast

Mynydd Perfedd

Elidir Fawr

start Llyn Ogwen

Foel-goch

A5

quarry

Y Garn

P

Tryfan

Llyn Peris

Gallt yr Ogof

YHA

Glyder Fawr

sta

LLANBERIS

Cwm Padrig

Glyder Fach

Y Foel Goch

inn

CAPEL CURIG

NANT PERIS

Nant Benglog and the East Ridges

A4086

A4086

Pass of Llanberis

Pen y Pass YHA

Pen y Gwryd Hotel

Dyffryn Mymbyr

cafe ■

Days out: the Glyderau

0   1 mile

1 kilometre

Days out: the Glyderau

Nant Ffrancon and the North-west Ridges

Start: Car park by Idwal Cottage Youth Hostel
  (GR: SH 649603)

Distance: 7 miles/11km

Height gain: 2620ft/800m

Time: 4–5 hours

Ogwen is bustling at most times of the day. Cars will be jostling for position in the limited parking spaces, and the take-away café will be selling Mars bars with steaming coffees and teas to walkers eager to grab some early refreshment before heading up the mountain paths. Beyond the pine trees, the Ogwen Falls will be thundering down the crags into Nant Ffrancon below, while tourists' cars speed by on their way to the coast.

But soon you're away from all this, heading along the wide Idwal Trail footpath, which begins from the left side of the toilet block

Below: The ledge path beneath the Mushroom Gardens, with Glyder Fach and Glyder Fawr in the distance.

Above: Y Garn seen from across Cwm Cywion.

and climbs into the cwm where it is said no bird will fly. The trail comes to the shores of Llyn Idwal. Many walkers will be content to walk around the lake, while the climbers will be making for those great slabs rising from the far shore. This route crosses the bridge over the outlet stream on the anti-clockwise path around the lake. Leave this path for a fainter one climbing grass slopes on the right.

Beyond a cross-wall the path gets serious and climbs steeply on to Y Garn's North-east Ridge. After briefly acquainting itself with Cwm Clyd, it swings right to rejoin the crest of the ridge. Strong walkers could make a detour to see the two corrie lakes if they've time, for they're idyllically sited and remote from the rest of the mountainside.

Unfortunately, the zigzag path up the steep

middle section of the ridge has been eroded by walkers' shortcuts, leaving a mess of gravelly scree. In the upper regions the ridge narrows, with exciting drops into Cwm Clyd and Cwm Cywion. On reaching a cairn on the main Glyder ridge, turn left to climb to Y Garn's summit.

Retrace your steps to the cairn before rounding Cwm Cywion, where two tiny pools lie in a secluded and seldom-visited hollow. At the col there is a path junction: the right fork stays close to the edge of the cwm climbing to Foel-goch's summit, while the left fork bypasses it on the left. If you don't like descents on scree slopes take the latter; if you want to see one of the best cliffs of the range, take the former. Both meet again near the pass of Bwlch y Brecan.

A fence guides the route to Foel-goch's summit. Divert to the eastern rim here to look down the immense cliffs of Creigiau Gleision. The cliffs continue beneath your feet and on Foel-goch's north-eastern ridge. Together they enclose Cwm Coch, the red corrie, where there's no lake but plenty of rugged atmosphere. Now you come to the screes. They're red and become increasingly loose as the path zigzags further down. At the bottom, the other side of the north-eastern ridge comes into view. The cliffs, divided by a notch and a narrow gulley, seldom see the sun and give Cwm Bual a sullen feel.

Ignore the first ladder stile on the right and continue along the ridge to the grassy col of Bwlch y Brecan, where craggy Elidir Fawr

looks extremely enticing. Unfortunately there's no time to explore it, so turn right over the ladder stile and descend on a little path that fades away on the grass spur separating Cwm Bual from Cwm Perfedd. To the right, beneath the cliffs of Foel-goch's north-eastern ridge and not far from the previously mentioned gulley, you should be able to pick out a ladder stile in a wall running beneath those cliffs. Make a beeline for it across a grassy depression.

The stile marks the start of a stony traverse path that follows the wall out of the cwm. It eventually swings right into Cwm Coch. The scenery is stunning as the path passes beneath cliffs. Tryfan is always dominant and there are glimpses of Llyn Idwal beyond Y Garn's rocky arms. Beyond Cwm Coch, the narrow path passes beneath the crags known as the Mushroom Gardens before coming into the lower regions of Cwm Cywion.

The path comes to an abrupt halt at Cywion's main stream. Scramble down the banks to ford the stream and follow the wall beyond its second gap. Now follow a very faint and intermittent path ESE down marshy, crag-interspersed hill slopes. Keep a look-out for a ladder stile in a cross-fence if in doubt, then aim for a cottage in the mid-distance. This is the Yr Hafod hostel, and the route reaches the old Nant Ffrancon road just to the left of it.

Turn left along the undulating road and follow it back to Ogwen and the start of the walk.

Nant Benglog and the East Ridges

Start: Car park behind Pinnacle Café,
    Capel Curig (GR: SH 720582)
Distance: 12½ miles/20km
Height gain: 3280ft/1000m
Time: 7–8 hours

If it's a weekend, get to the car park early because it soon becomes full. You can always have your breakfast at the Pinnacle Café after you've claimed your space. The stony track at the back of the car park was once the main road through the Llugwy and Ogwen valleys before Thomas Telford engineered the famous London–Holyhead highway (now the A5).

It takes the route past Gelli farm, beyond which another track joins in from the left. It is at this point you must leave the track to climb the hill slopes on the left, threading through grassy gaps between the rocky outcrops on to the grassy Glyder ridge. Traces of a path are faint and intermittent in the early stages. To the left Moel Siabod fills the picture with its featureless northern slopes towering above the Mymbyr lakes. On the other side of the ridge across the Llugwy valley the pointed peak of Pen yr Llithrig y Wrach rises in sweeping grassy slopes.

The path finally establishes itself on Cefn y Capel. It wanders mostly on the southern side of the ridge, which is for now bare and grassy.

Below: The Cantilever on Glyder Fach's summit.

Occasionally it crosses over to give views of the Carneddau. By now the long Cowlyd Reservoir has come into view, sitting uneasily beneath the rocky slopes of Creigiau Gleision and those of Pen Llithrig y Wrach.

Soon the dark cliffs of Gallt yr Ogof peer over undulations in the grass ridge. The gradient gets steeper and beyond a cross-wall the path climbs in earnest towards the summit. At the last moment it veers left to traverse the southern flanks. However, getting to the top of Gallt yr Ogof is only a matter of clambering over those boulders. The summit rocks offer several airy perches to view Ogwen. Tryfan, Glyder Fach's Bristly Ridge and Pen yr Ole Wen have been added to the view and serve to urge the walker to proceed in haste from this pleasant vantage point to the more spectacular places that lie ahead.

By descending west along the craggy ridge, the original path can be rejoined. Once again this shy path tries to miss out a peak, this time Y Foel Goch. Again aim for the crags of the summit. Tryfan now dominates all, lying beyond a wild cwm of heather, scree and dark crag. Looking across the cwm you can see the old miners' track straddling Bwlch Tryfan and easing across the screes beneath the jagged rocks of Bristly Ridge. What a journey to work! It's better than the M6 motorway, but I bet they had to get up early to get to the copper mines of Snowdon on time.

Now it's a simple descent on grass down to meet the miners' route at a grassy col where the shallow pools of Caseg-fraith languish beneath Gyder Fach's stark eastern flank. The peaty path of the col becomes increasingly rough as it climbs alongside the rim of Cwm Tryfan. Eventually the path comes to Glyder Fach's upper boulder slopes, where walkers have to clamber across a cairned route to the summit plateau. The spiky upper crest of Bristly Ridge can be seen on the right with excited walkers coming off it, some with pleasure, others with relief. The Cantilever, a great horizontal rock slab pivoted on vertical outcrops, is like a film set, with camera operators below and real rock stars perched on the slab.

Heading west past the huge but otherwise uninteresting pile of rocks that form the summit, the route comes to Castell y Gwynt, a jagged rampart that guards the mountain's west end. Here a path descends to the left of the 'castle' but ends among huge boulders – there's more clambering to be done, this time down to the pass of Bwlch y Ddwy Glyder.

The going gets much easier from here, on a gently graded cairned path to Glyder Fawr. However, to get the best out of Glyder Fawr, it is better to stick to the north rim around Cwm Bochlwyd, where you'll be able to look down the rocky spur of Cribin to Llyn Bochlwyd. Beyond Gribin, Cwm Cneifion has no lake but it has an equally impressive rocky spur known as the Seniors' Ridge. By this time the main path has been rejoined as it threads between the spiky outcrops of Glyder Fawr's summit plateau, each one pretending to be the highest place.

The cairned path continues to the eastern edge of the plateau where an unpleasantly loose winding path descends to Llyn y Cwn, which lies in a grassy hollow beneath Y Garn's sprawling grass ridge.

Follow the path around the right side of the tarn before turning right on a clear path to the north rim. Here the scene transforms again as the path now dives off the edge to rake down in slabs and boulders into the hollow of Cwm Idwal. To the left there's a great dark cleft in the cliffs at the back of the cwm: it's called Twll Du, which means the black fracture, but is far better known as the Devil's Kitchen.

The base-rich soils on the surrounding ledges have allowed many species of arctic plants to flourish. The most famous, the rare Snowdon Lily, was discovered in the 17th century by Edward Llwyd. Tufted and arctic saxifrage are here but hard to spot, but the starry and mossy saxifrages are here for all to see, as are wood sorrel, wood anemone and oak ferns. The foliage seems to flow down the rocks and you can see why its alternative name is the Hanging Gardens.

On reaching the bottom of the cwm there are paths either side of its lake, Llyn Idwal.

The rougher one goes right, beneath the diagonal climbing crags known as the Idwal Slabs, while the one on the left beneath Y Garn's south-eastern ridge is more direct. Both routes meet at the footbridge across the lake's outflow and continue on a wide engineered path down to Ogwen where, if it's not too late, you might be able to buy tea and cake.

To get back to the start of the walk you could go cross-country south of the road, but the ground is quite rough for this time of the day. There are pavements all along the roadside by the shores of Llyn Ogwen. Beyond Tryfan's North Ridge, opposite the entrance to Glan Dena, leave the road for a stony track on the left, which is the other end of the 'old road' you were on earlier in the day. Follow this beneath the mimicking Tryfan Bach, and both Gwern Gof farms. The relatively flat track makes a fitting end to the day, as you pass below the buttresses of Gallt yr Ogof. The cave referred to in its name lies a quarter of the way up the crags to the left of a large gulley. After 3½ miles/5.5km, the track returns to the car park at Capel Curig.

Opposite: On Tryfan's summit rocks (photograph by Nicola Gillham).

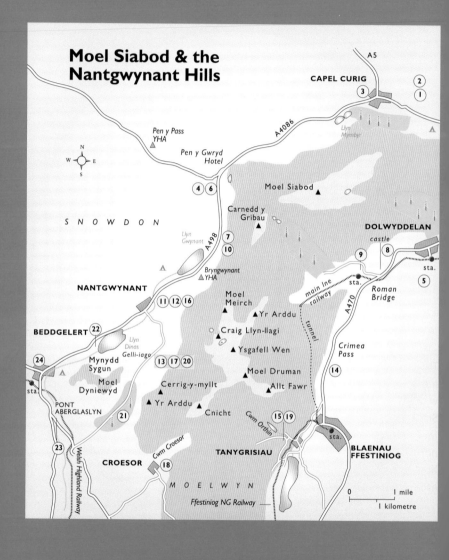

Moel Siabod & the Nantgwynant Hills

CAPEL CURIG

A5

② ①

③

Pen y Pass
YHA

Pen y Gwryd
Hotel

A4086

Llyn
Mymbyr

N
W   E
S

④ ⑥

Moel Siabod ▲

Carnedd y
Gribau
▲

DOLWYDDELAN

S N O W D O N

Llyn
Gwynant

A498

⑦
⑩

castle

⑧

sta.

⑨

Bryngwynant
YHA

NANTGWYNANT

Moel
Meirch
▲

▲ Yr Arddu

main lne
railway

sta.

Roman
Bridge

⑤

⑪ ⑫ ⑯

Craig Llyn-llagi
▲

▲ Ysgafell Wen

A470

Crimea
Pass

BEDDGELERT ㉒

Llyn
Dinas

Gelli-iago

⑬ ⑰ ⑳

Moel Druman
▲

Allt Fawr
▲

⑭

㉔

Mynydd
Sygun

Cerrig-y-myllt
▲

tunnel

Moel
Dyniewyd

▲ Yr Arddu

Cnicht
▲

Cwm Orthin

⑮ ⑲

sta.

**BLAENAU
FFESTINIOG**

**PONT
ABERGLASLYN**

㉑

TANYGRISIAU

㉓

Welsh Highland Railway

Cwm Croesor

㉘

Cwm Croesor

CROESOR

M O E L W Y N

Ffestiniog NG Railway

0   1 mile
        1 kilometre

Although Moel Siabod lies just across the Nantgwynant and Nant Gwryd valleys from Snowdon and the Glyderau mountains, it's isolated from other peaks, so much so that authors often lump it with the Moelwynion for convenience. But Siabod shares nothing with those peaks. The deep chasms of Cwm Croesor and Cwmorthin seem to end any connections there might have been, both geologically and spiritually. The Moelwynion belong in the slate world of Ffestiniog and that's where I've put them.

THE PEAKS

Main Tops	height	
Moel Siabod	2860ft	872m
Allt Fawr	2290ft	698m
Cnicht	2260ft	689m
Ysgafell Wen	2204ft	672m
Moel Meirch	1990ft	607m
Craig Llyn-llagi	1950ft	595m
Carnedd y Gribau	1938ft	591m
Yr Arddu		
(Lledr Valley)	1933ft	589m
Cerrig-y-myllt	1518ft	463m
Yr Arddu (Nantmor)	1275ft	389m
Mynydd Dyniewyd	1254ft	382m
Mynydd Sygun	1049ft	320m

The Nantgwynant and Lledr valleys are among the prettiest in Snowdonia. The fine mountain scenery is embellished by oak woods, enchanting river scenery with waterfalls and peaceful tree-overhung calm stretches such as the Fairy Glen. Moel Siabod and Cnicht, respectively the northern and southern outliers, play a large part in the mountainscapes of the valleys. Siabod has two fine rocky ridges, the knobbly north ridge and Daear Fawr, an exciting rocky arête with a hint of a scramble. Its bouldery summit offers some of the best views in Wales, including one showing every last detail of the Snowdon Horseshoe.

Carnedd y Cribau, rising from the southern arm of Moel Siabod, has a nice crag and short grass summit complete with a small pool – and, with the craggy arm of Cefnycerrig rising from the Pen y Gwryd Inn almost to the summit, it's rather like a mini-Siabod. However, the terrain changes radically beyond the high pass of Bwlch

Rhediad. Here, Moel Meirch rises in the unkempt and random fashion of a Rhinog peak, with rugged crags tangled with tussocky heather.

The Nantgwynant hills as a whole offer wondrous journeys, through the oak woods of the lower slopes, and along the shorelines of secretive tarns that reflect the rocky summit crags and bluffs to perfection. The stretch between Moel Meirch and Cnicht provides some of the best ridge-walking in Wales. There are more delectable wild camping sites here than anywhere else I know.

Perhaps the finest Nantgwynant approaches are the ones that take in Llyn Llagi, a circular tarn surrounded by splendid cliffs whose expanse is briefly interrupted by a cascade fed by the waters of Llyn yr Adar 180m above. Cnicht or Ysgafell Wen, or both, are the usual destinations. Another lake, Llyn Edno, basks in a shallow, heathery basin between Moel Meirch, Ysgafell Wen and a third subsidiary ridge, Yr Arddu. Yr Arddu runs north-east to the Lledr Valley displaying graceful flanks of heather and crag, which capture attention when seen from the wild Crimea Pass.

The enjoyment of approaches made from the Lledr Valley to Moel Siabod and the Nantgwynant hills is heightened by a detour to see Dolwyddelan Castle, built by Llewelyn the Great some time in the 13th century. Today the castle is in ruins, not much more than a square tower and some crumbling battlements, but the wild mountain setting lends a superb drama to its situation. It is believed that an earlier castle (Tomen Castell), sited nearer the river in the village, was the birthplace of that celebrated Prince of Wales.

Cnicht, like Siabod, has a hard heart of Ordovician crag, but its summit ridge is soft with short-cropped grass punctuated by three rocky bluffs. With picnic spots galore, it has a view with scores of little lakes, some set on the high ridges and plateaux, and others in little corries beneath. Its gentle nature comes to an abrupt halt on the face overlooking Cwm Croesor, for a great rocky ridge plunges in precipitous scree slopes into the valley floor several hundred feet below.

Tucked away among the green fields at the mouth of Cwm Croesor lies the tiny village sharing the same name. Unusually for a place so small and isolated, Croesor still has its school, though the chapel has been converted and there is no shop. Unsurprisingly, given the spectacular scenery of the cwm, this is the most popular way to Cnicht and the ridge makes an exhilarating finale.

Opposite: Climbing the east ridge of Moel Siabod with Llyn y Foel far below.

Moel Siabod, pronounced 'moyle sharbod', meaning the crooked bare hill, is a complex character with many sides to its nature. If you're driving from England along the A5, Moel Siabod will be the first big Snowdonian you'll come across.

From here it towers above the forests, high pastures and old slate quarries of Betws y Coed with a rugged ridge of knobbly crag. Siabod even manages to block out Snowdon until you round the corner to the twin lakes of Mymbyr. From here all eyes are on Snowdon, and Moel Siabod languishes into its dull weekday suit. Across the spartan shores of the lakes and above a dull, inky spruce forest, its slopes of moor grass, etched with sparse crag in the mid regions, rise in simple but monotonous fashion to a slightly ruffled rock crest.

It's from the Lledr Valley that the true splendour and dignity of Moel Siabod reveals itself. The spruce forests still cloak the valley but the skyline is filled with bold crag topping a fascinating complex of heathery rock knolls. The north ridge can be seen climbing to the pointed summit, but now a splendid arête, Daear Fawr, is added. Together they form a corrie ringed with shadowy buttresses and gulleys.

In there somewhere, but out of sight from the valley floor, lies the large corrie lake, Llyn y Foel. Although not the most popular route (that claim belongs to the approach from Pont Cyfyng), the approaches from Dolwyddelan are the most stimulating. Daear Ddu is pure pleasure. The rock is firm with plenty of hand- and footholds, and places on the left-hand side to avoid the difficulties you don't fancy tackling.

Moel Siabod's summit is all rock, as those who come by way of the bouldery north-east ridge will testify, and its isolation from other major peaks pays dividends. When you're on top of Siabod you're in the gods, and the cast on the stage includes the Snowdon Horseshoe, backed up by the Glyderau and Carneddau; the Moelwynion, seen across a long ridge of heather and rocky bluffs; while across the glinting waters of Trawsfynydd's lake the gnarled outlines of the Rhinog mountains form the backdrop.

Opposite: Moel Siabod from the south (photograph by Nicola Gillham).

Route MSN1
Llyn y Foel and the East Ridge
The most popular route with a fine finale
Start: Pont Cyfyng (GR: SH 734571)
Distance: 3 miles/5km
Height gain: 2395ft/730m
Time: 2 hours

Follow the lane southwards over the bridge and past some cottages before taking the second signed footpath on the right, which follows a farm lane past more cottages. Take the diversion from the lane to avoid Rhos farmhouse before rejoining it further up the hillside. The lane becomes a path, traversing sombre moorland before coming to an unnamed lake at the foot of Siabod's north-east ridge. Stay with the main path keeping the ridge to the right.

Beyond the derelict barracks of the Rhos quarries the path skirts a deep quarry pool before climbing more peaty slopes to a shelf overlooking Llyn y Foel, a huge tarn ringed with crags and gulleys. After traversing marshy ground to the right of the tarn, the path comes to Siabod's rocky east ridge, Daear Ddu – an exhilarating but easy scramble to the summit. There's easier ground to the left for those who don't like the excitement of the ridge. The ridge ends all too soon on the summit plateau, just north-east of the trig point.

Route MSN2
The North-east Ridge
A bit of a slog over the boulders of the high north-east ridge
Start: Pont Cyfyng (GR: SH 734571)
Distance: 2¼ miles/4.5km
Height gain: 2395ft/730m
Time: 2 hours

As in Route MSN1 follow the lane southwards over the bridge, take the second footpath on the right, a farm lane climbing past some cottages and take the signed diversion to avoid Rhos farm. The path rejoins the lane higher up and climbs past the derelict barracks of Rhos quarry.

At GR 724558, just short of the unnamed lake, climb right to follow the rocky north-east ridge, which can be followed all the way to the summit. The going gets harder as the route crosses bouldery ground, but views towards Snowdon and the Glyderau compensate.

Note: there is easier ground on the hill slopes to the right of the boulders.

Opposite: Moel Siabod from above Pont Cyfyng, Capel Curig.

234

Moel Siabod

Daear Ddu

Llyn y Foel

old quarry

MSN1

MSN2

MSN1/2

old quarry barracks

link route

Pont Cyfyng

A5

Afon Llugwy

inn

Snowdon (Yr Wyddfa)

Llynnau Mymbyr

Plas y Brenin

Cobdens (hotel)

Capel Curig

Route MSN3

Capel Curig and Plas y Brenin

A steady plod highlighted by great views
of Snowdon

Start: Car park behind Pinnacle Café
   (GR: SH 720582)

Distance: 3 miles/5km

Height gain: 2265ft/690m

Time: 2 hours

Take the track from the back of the car park leading away from Capel Curig, then turn left on the track at Gelli farm. This leads to the road opposite Llynnau Mymbyr. Turn left along the road towards the Plas y Brenin outdoor centre before, just short of the complex, turning right on a path leading over the footbridge spanning Nant Gwryd at the point the stream filters into Llynnau Mymbyr.

On the far side cut across a wide forestry road to climb on a path through coniferous woodland. On meeting another forestry road turn left for a few paces, then climb right on a narrow path that eventually leaves the forest to emerge on to the hillside. From here it climbs by the side of higher pine woodland with a tumbling stream to the right. Looking back there are tremendous views of the eastern Carneddau, with Pen Llithrig y Wrach and Creigiau Gleision being particularly dominating from behind the shoulder of the splintered northern end of the Glyder ridge and the rooftops of Capel Curig.

After raking up the peat and grass slopes high on Siabod's north-west flanks, the path all but fades away, but by maintaining your direction the summit will soon be reached.

Moel
Siabod

MSN3

Llynnau Mymbyr

Plas y Brenin

P
cafe
Gelli

Capel Curig

Route MSN4
Pen y Gwryd and Cefnycerrig

*Seldom-used and marshy at the start; nice
    views of Nantgwynant*

Start: Roadside car parking opposite Pen
    y Gwryd (GR: SH 659557)

Distance: 3½ miles/5.5km

Height gain: 1970ft/600m

Time: 2–2½ hours

A ladder stile on the eastern side of the Beddgelert road (A498) by the Pen y Gwryd Hotel
allows entry to the marshy land by Llyn Lock-
wood. After traversing the northern slopes of
the small hill overlooking the lake, head
south-east across rushy ground to cross Nant-
y-llys for Cefnycerrig's lowest crags. The route
now follows a fence to the ridge at Bwlch

Above: Moel Siabod seen across Crimea Pass.

Rhiw'r Ychen, a narrow pass guarded by vegetated crags overlooking Llynnau Diwaunydd. Turn left here and follow the fence up
the grass of Siabod's west ridge. The views
across Nantgwynant to Snowdon and its
horseshoe route improve with every step.

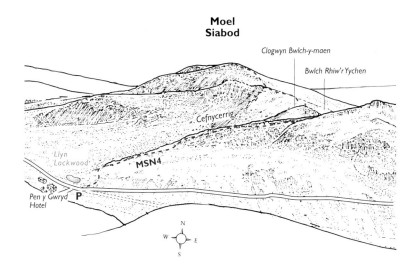

Route MSN5
Dolwyddelan and Llyn y Foel
The back-door route; nice finish
Start: Picnic site, Dolwyddelan
(GR: SH 738522)
Distance: 3 miles/5km
Height gain: 2395ft/730m
Time: 2–2½ hours

Follow the road back to the village, then turn half-right on a path cutting diagonally across the playing fields to reach the main road. A tarmac lane, staggered to the right, climbs steeply between buildings on the far side of the road. Veering right, it soon becomes a cart track enclosed by scrub woodland and mossy walls.

The track meets a forestry road joining from the right and follows it northwards through conifers fronted by stands of deciduous trees. This makes the forest rather lighter and more spacious than many of the dense Sitka spruce plantations, a feeling enhanced by recent tree felling which allows superb views of Siabod's craggy south-east face – for now!

Stay with the flinted main road as it crosses, then recrosses, the Afon Ystumiau. Just beyond the second crossing the road divides – a point marked by a signpost. Turn left following the direction sign for Moel Siabod. The winding track ends at a wooden footbridge. Beyond this a narrow but clear stony path climbs over sinuous tree roots to a stile at the forest's edge – the waterfall here is quite spectacular after snows or heavy rain. Now the narrow path climbs rough slopes of crag, heather and bracken.

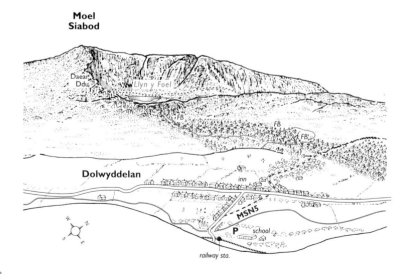

Above: Moel Siabod from Dolyddelan, showing the Daear Ddu Ridge (left) and the shady cwm of Llyn Foel.

Threading through the craggy bluffs the little path comes to the dam of Llyn y Foel. Turn left here to round the large corrie lake to reach the foot of Daear Ddu. The ascent involves some easy scrambling, but unless wintry conditions prevail it's quite safe. For those who don't like too much excitement there's easier ground to the left of the crest. Either way you will reach the mountain's magnificent summit.

Other route options

It is feasible to start at the Dolwyddelan Castle car park and follow the public footpaths behind the castle to Blaenau Dolwyddelan before climbing by the forest to the un-named tarn at GR 697531. A dull plod would then continue by the eastern edge of the forest before striking out northwards by the fence towards Craig Ddu. After climbing between breaks in the crag a pathless course NNE (still by the fence) would lead to the summit.

RIDGE ROUTE

Carnedd y Gribau
Distance: 2¼ miles/3.6km
Height gain: 250ft/75m
Time: 1 hour

From the summit, head west on a grassy ridge, descending alongside a fence down to Bwlch Clorad, where there's a brief climb to the rock knuckle of Clogwyn Bwlch-y-maen before descending and angling right down to Bwlch Rhiw'r Ychen, a narrow rocky pass used by ancient travellers between Pen y Gwryd and Dolwyddelan. Here, you'll be looking down impressive cliffs to the conifer-surrounded, egg-timer-shaped lake of Llynnau Diwaunydd (the lake is in the plural because it becomes two during very dry periods).

From the pass, a path bordered by the ridge fence twists amongst bilberry and boulders on a steep but short pull to the airy summit of Carnedd y Gribau.

Opposite: Moel Siabod from Dolwyddelan Castle.
Below: A storm brewing over Moel Siabod and Llynnau Mymbyr.

CARNEDD Y GRIBAU

Check out the famous view from the summit of Snowdon across Cwm Dyli and the cliffs of Y Lliwedd. Carnedd y Gribau's always there – it's the craggy one to the right of Moel Siabod – but nobody notices. They should, for Carnedd y Gribau has a nice craggy ridge, Cefnycerrig; its own lake, and some exciting cliffs. The trouble with Carnedd y Cribau is its height. Next to Siabod and Snowdon, it's a pygmy of a hill and, to compound matters, it misses out on being a 2000-footer by just over 60 feet. Although mathematics has no part to play for the mountain connoisseur, to the peak-bagger it keeps this mountain from the tick lists.

This saddle-backed, crag-topped peak has its finest face on the east, where a deep fringe of dark vegetated cliffs spans the slopes between the passes of Bwlch Rhediad and Bwlch Rhiw'r Ychen – the cliffs surrounding the shady cwm cradling Llynnau Diwaunydd are particularly impressive. While the eastern side's stark wildness is spoiled slightly by plantations of spruce and larch, no such thing can be said about the western slopes, for these are a fine complex of rocky gorge and oak woods, rising from the Glaslyn river. Climbs from this side are shorter, steeper and memorable.

I've wild camped a couple of times on Carnedd y Gribau, not far from a rock-shaded summit pool. I've watched a summer sun sink behind Snowdon, bathing it with pink and orange, and I've watched it rise next morning to give a crisp golden glow to the Moelwyn and Siabod ridges. You must give Carnedd y Gribau a chance and take in the ever-changing ridge scenery from here to Cnicht. Or include it in a Siabod itinerary, but it's not to be missed.

Opposite: Carnedd y Gribau from Coed Mawr.
Left: Carnedd y Gribau from the slopes of Yr Arddu.

Route MSN6

Pen y Gwryd and Cefnycerrig

A pleasant climb after a boggy start

Start: Lay-by, Pen y Gwryd (GR: SH 660557)

Distance: 2 miles /3.3km

Height gain: 1080ft/330m

Time: 1¼ hours

A ladder stile on the eastern side of the Bedd-gelert road (A498) by the Pen y Gwryd Hotel allows entry to the marshy land by Llyn Lock-wood. After traversing the northern slopes of the small hill overlooking the lake, head south-east across rushy ground to cross Nant-y-llys. Although you could follow Route MSN4 up Cefnycerrig's ridge, it is better to head south-east towards the little craggy gorge cut by the Nant-y-llys. Although there's no path, the terrain improves to one of short, sheep-cut grass and crag as the little gorge leads up the hillside. The course eventually leads to Bwlch Rhiw'r Ychen, a narrow rocky pass at the foot of Siabod's west ridge, where mossy crags plummet to Llynnau Diwaun-ydd.

From the pass, climb right alongside the ridge-fence on a narrow path meandering through steep slopes of bilberry and boulders to reach the summit of Carnedd y Gribau.

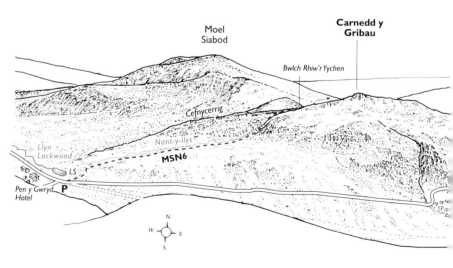

Route MSN7
Nantgwynant and Bwlch Rhediad

Quiet but very pleasant route taking in a
*   splendid outlying summit*
Start: Lay-by (GR: SH 656527)
Distance: 3¼ miles/6km
Height gain: 2850ft/870m
Time: 2½–3 hours

A waymarked footpath climbs into some delightful deciduous woodland, and the steep and winding stony path soon enters hillsides of rocky bluffs. The views back to Nantgwynant are stunningly beautiful, with Llyn Gwynant usually reflecting the pyramid of Yr Aran and the surrounding woodland to perfection.

After passing a ruined shepherd's hut, a gate allows passage through the tall intake wall. The path climbs through increasingly wilder terrain until it reaches the grassy col of Bwlch y Rhediad. After the beauty of Nantgwynant you're now confronted by an altogether more sombre scene, as you look over the shoulder of Yr Arddu, across the rugged moorland and conifer forest of Cwm Edno towards the mountains of Ffestiniog and the Crimea Pass.

Climb left from the pass over more rocky bluffs to reach Carnedd y Gribau's summit.

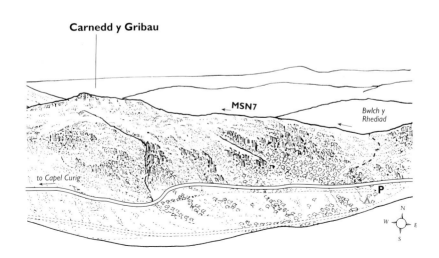

Carnedd y Gribau

MSN7

Bwlch y Rhediad

to Capel Curig

P

Above: On the descent from Bwlch Rhediad to Nantgwynant, with Moel Hebog and Yr Aran forming a backdrop to the calm waters of Llyn Gwynant.

Route MSN8
Coed Mawr and Bwlch Rhediad

Stimulating route past an old castle and fine outlying peak

Start: Lay-by west of Dolwyddelan
    (GR: SH 725523)
Distance: 8 miles/12km
Height gain: 2790ft/850m
Time: 5 hours

From the lay-by, walk westwards up the road then follow an enclosed track on the right signed to Dolwyddelan Castle. Take the right fork above the ticket office and stay with the track as it passes to the right of the castle. (Note: if you want to visit the castle you need to pay at the ticket office.)

Ignore the track where it turns right and go straight ahead on a less well-defined track climbing a hollow between craggy knolls. The track comes down to a minor road by some farm buildings at Pen y Rhiw. Turn right here towards Blaenau Dolwyddelan, passing beneath a conifer plantation. Just beyond a river crossing, take the right fork towards Coed Mawr then fork right again by the farm on a track climbing the hillsides on the north side of the valley.

Close to the terminus of the track, turn off right on a footpath crossing a footbridge over a stream before heading for a copse of conifers. Here you join another footpath that heads westwards to reach the pass, Bwlch y Rhediad. Join Route MSN7 and climb left up the craggy ridge to the summit.

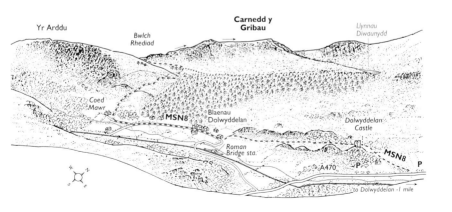

Other route options

It is possible to follow the footpath from Blaen Dolwyddelan to the edge of the conifer forest then follow the eastern perimeter of the plantation past the unnamed lake to the shores of Llynnau Diwaunydd. A grassy rake between crags leads up to Bwlch Rhiw'r Ychen – it's very steep, but safe in dry conditions. Here you would climb south as in Route MSN7 on the climb among rock outcrops to the summit.

RIDGE ROUTES

Moel Siabod

Distance: 2¼ miles/3.6km
Height gain: 1250ft/ 380m
Time: 1½ hours

Descend the steep little path by the fence down to Bwlch Rhiw'r Ychen and climb to the rocky knoll of Clogwyn Bwlch-y-maen. After dropping to a shallow col, the broad grassy west ridge leads to the summit of Moel Siabod.

Moel Meirch

Distance: 2½ miles/4km
Height gain: 850ft/ 260m
Time: 1–1½ hours

Descend south-west down a ridge of rock outcrops and moor grass to reach Bwlch Rhediad where you climb the slopes of Cerrig Cochion with a fence to the left.

The route encounters a couple of boggy sections, but stiles in the fence allow detours on firmer ground. On reaching the ridge's highest ground climb right on a narrow path weaving through rock and heather to reach Moel Meirch's craggy summit.

Left: Dolwyddelan Castle.
Opposite: Carnedd y Gribau from its southern ridge.

YR ARDDU
(LLEDR VALLEY)

This, the more northerly of two hills known as Yr Arddu, stretches north-east from the main Siabod–Nantgwynant ridge near Llyn Edno and separates the lonely Cwm Edno and the upper valley of the Afon Lledr. It's a broad whale-backed ridge whose tufted grass and heather terrain is liberally studded with crag and outcrop and decorated by the odd shallow pool.

Seen from the Crimea Pass road above Dol-wyddelan and the upper Lledr Valley, you can see why Yr Arddu gets its name, which means the darkness, for unless it's morning its grace-fully arced crags are often in shadow. This is the way to tackle the hill for a truly satisfying approach.

The facts that it's off the beaten track, its summit fails to achieve the magic 2000ft height, and there are no recognised footpaths means that Yr Arddu gets few visitors. That can be a blessing, for intrepid walkers who toil up those initially steep grass slopes will be rewarded by a sense of open space unadulterated by the plough, the path engi-neer or the Coke-can-and-orange-peel dis-posal merchant. This is how hills used to be.

Left: Looking across the upper Lledr Valley from Yr Arddu.

Route MSN9

Coed Mawr

Stimulating

Start: Roman Bridge station, Dolwyddelan –
   there's parking for a few cars where the
   road widens beyond the bridge
   (GR: SH 712516)

Distance: 3¼ miles/6km

Height gain: 1480ft/450m

Time: 2 hours

Follow the narrow winding lane up the Lledr
Valley, over the bridge and past the pleasant
hamlet of Blaenau Dolwyddelan. Just beyond
the forest and a river crossing, take the right
fork towards Coed Mawr, then fork right
again by the farm on a track signed to Nantgwynant. This climbs hillsides on the north
side of the valley over pastures dotted with
gorse and dominated by the graceful craggy
slopes of Yr Arddu's east face. The track soon
enters the wide moorland cwm of Ceunant
Ty'n-y-ddol, a stream that is soon engulfed by
the conifers of the lower valley.

On passing through a gate nearly level
with the south-west tip of the conifers, leave
the track and strike up left by the wall. Sheep-
tracks promise little and deliver less but can
help for short stretches over the rough grassland terrain. The wall leads to the top edge of
Yr Arddu's eastern crags where the going
becomes easier. Views are now dominated by
the Lledr Valley.

Behind you are verdant pastures; ahead is
wilderness at the head of the cwm, where the
crinkle-cut ridges of Allt Fawr, Moel Druman
and Ysgafell Wen are dark and brooding. A
little path soon develops and takes the route
through crag and boulder, among heather,
bilberry and mosses to a fine summit where
a small cairn is piled on top of weather-
smoothed rocks.

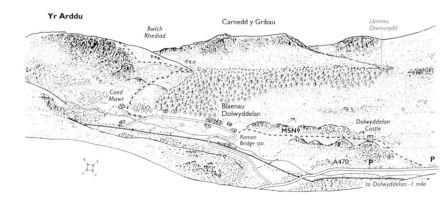

Other route options

The other logical route would start at the Britannia Car Park, Nantgwynant (that's the Watkin Path car park), or Gelli-iago on the Nantmor Road above Nantgwynant, and follow the right of way through the cwm of the Afon Llynedno to Llyn Edno. After going over the ladder stile by the far shores of the lake a short trek north-eastwards across a marshy hollow would lead to Yr Arddu's rocky ridge.

RIDGE ROUTE

Moel Meirch

Distance: 1¼ miles/2km
Height gain: 210ft/ 65m
Time: 40 minutes

From the cairn on the summit, head southwest along the broad rock-studded ridge between two shallow pools and towards the distant Llyn Edno. The route comes to a marshy bowl as Llyn Edno temporarily disappears beneath the horizon. The rocky ridge hereabouts starts rising left towards Ysgafell Wen but, to avoid unnecessary ascent, keep to the right edge of the crags just above the marshes. Llyn Edno and the main Nantgwynant–Siabod ridge fence re-appear and a ladder stile behind a squat crag allows you to cross to the other side. Turn right then follow the narrow left fork path climbing among heather and crag to Moel Meirch's summit rocks.

Above: Climbing the north slopes of Yr Arddu.

Moel Meirch is a fascinating maze of rounded knolls formed from splintered rhyolitic tuffs cloaked with heather and culminating in a summit ruffled by half a mile of jagged crags. Seen from Nantgwynant, its slopes are interspersed with woods of oak and mountain ash, and rent by little gorges of fast-flowing streams. Anyone with affection for the Rhinogydd mountains near Harlech will feel the same about Moel Meirch, for it has the same rugged feel to it.

Like Carnedd y Gribau, Moel Meirch just fails to reach the 2000ft mark (by 10 feet), although baggers of 600m peaks have it on their lists. As would be expected on such terrain, most of Moel Meirch's 607 metres are hard metres. Paths often fade into the heather or patches of marsh. But there's fun to be had, clambering over rocks, pausing for those breathtaking views across the valley to Snowdon, and admiring the delicate pinks of bogbean in small secluded pools.

Llyn Edno, to the south of the summit, is a stunningly beautiful, rock-bound tarn shared with neighbouring Ysgafell Wen. It is the source of the stream that flows into the wild Cwm Edno before joining the Lledr near Dolwyddelan. Approach Moel Meirch from Cwm Edno and I can almost guarantee you a people-free day until you reach the ridge.

Opposite: Moel Meirch summit, looking to Snowdon. Right: Moel Meirch seen across Llyn Dinas.

Route MSN10
Bwlch Rhediad

Quiet but very pleasant route taking in a splendid outlying summit

Start: Lay-by on A498 1 mile/1.6km NW of Llyn Gwynant (GR: SH 656527)

Distance: 3¼ miles/6km

Height gain: 2850ft/870m

Time: 2½ –3 hours

A waymarked footpath on the opposite side of the road from the car park climbs into some delightful deciduous woodland. A steep and winding stony path continues to the top of the woods and passes an old ruined shepherd's cottage before continuing through wild craggy hillside. Beyond a gate in the intake wall the path climbs through wind-swept grass mountainside to reach the pass of Bwlch Rhediad, where you look across the desolate moorland of Cwm Edno towards the hills of Ffestiniog and the Crimea Pass.

Now climb right by a ridge fence to the rugged Cerrig Cochion ridge and on the rim of Cwm Edno. The route comes across a couple of boggy sections on the ridge of Cerrig Cochion, but stiles in the fence allow detours on slightly firmer ground. As the path reaches its highest point, leave it to veer right along a narrow path through heather and bilberry.

After a short distance of crag-hopping you come to the highest rocks, where you can admire the view of Snowdon, Siabod and the Moelwynion.

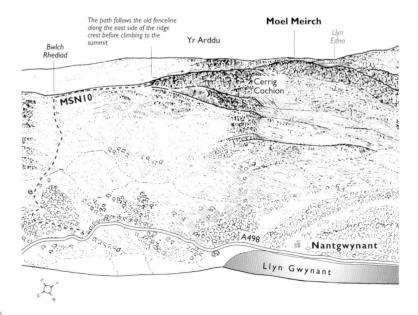

The path follows the old fenceline along the east side of the ridge crest before climbing to the summit

Bwlch Rhediad

Yr Arddu

Moel Meirch

Llyn Edno

MSN10

Cerrig Cochion

A498

Nantgwynant

Llyn Gwynant

Route MSN11
Nantgwynant and Llyn Edno

*Quiet route which is quite hard to navigate
in the middle stretches*

Start: Britannia car park, Nantgwynant
(GR: SH 628507)
Distance: 3½ miles/5.6km
Height gain: 1970ft/600m
Time: 2½ hours

From the north end of the car park, follow
Plas Gwynant's tarmac drive before taking
the left fork, a stony track through the woodlands north of the main buildings. A footpath
waymarker points the way and a delightful
path, cushioned by rhododendron leaves,
descends through woodland, across the
foaming Afon Llynedno, and out on to the
narrow tarmac Nantmor Lane.

Turn left along the lane, uphill to the sharp
right-hand bend at the top. Here go through
the right of two gates and follow a zizag stony
track towards Hafodydd Brithion farm. Just
short of the farm a signposted stony track on
the right climbs to a very wet meadow. Here,
cross the stream and the meadow before continuing the climb with a stone wall on the left
and woodland to the right. Beyond a gate the
path comes upon a ruin. Look right here.
Beneath a large tree, a concrete waymarking
posts sets the direction, NNE across more wet
fields to a ladder stile at the edge of the rocky
foothills.

Over the ladder stile, follow the wall left.

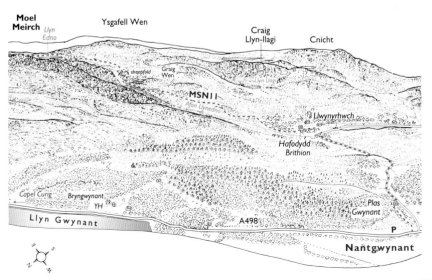

The path takes you into an enclosure of rock walls, both man-made and natural. A gap at the top allows the path on to the hillsides overlooking the bustling Afon Llynedno. Many walkers follow the banks of the river from here, but it is better to use the faint track that climbs the rocky hillsides to the right. The path seems to end at the base of some tiered crags, but you will be able to pick your way through a weakness in them.

The path re-establishes itself on a wet grassy shelf of rock and gradually veers east. By now Moel Meirch's ruffled crest and heather-clad bluffs dominate the wild rocky cwm. The river tumbles down in a series of cataracts and waterfalls, its course decorated in the lower reaches by thickets of rhododendron.

Higher up the river splits up into a series of streams and the path comes to a large sheepfold (GR 656497). To find your way up to Llyn Edno (the lake), you'll need to cross a stream beyond the sheepfold, before climbing southeast, then east on trackless slopes close to the lake's outflow stream.

On reaching the lake, follow its northern shores to reach the Moelwyn ridge fence, then turn left to climb by the fence for a short way before forking left on a narrow path, which climbs rough slopes of heather, crag and bilberry to reach the rocky summit.

Other route options

It is perfectly feasible, although rough and pathless in the mid-regions, to follow the bridleway track from Blaenau Dolwyddelan and Coed Mawr but leave it to enter Cwm Edno. The stream would lead out of the cwm to the shores of Llyn Edno, where you could join Route MSN11.

RIDGE ROUTES

Carnedd y Gribau

Distance: 2¼ miles/4km
Height gain: 840ft/ 255m
Time: 1–1½ hours

From the summit follow the narrow path eastwards over rocks, heather and bilberry to reach the ridge fence. Turn left here. Any marshy patches can be avoided by going over stiles in the ridge fence to terra firma. In general the route keeps to the Cwm Edno side of the ridge as it continues over Cerrig Cochion. After descending to the grassy hollow of Bwlch Rhediad, the route climbs among rocky bluffs to the summit of Carnedd y Gribau, easily recognised by its small summit pool.

Ysgafell Wen (South Summit)

Distance: 1¼ miles/2.8km
Height gain: 540ft/ 165m
Time: 1 hour

Again to return to the ridge fence follow the narrow path eastwards from the summit, over rocks, heather and bilberry. Turn right and descend to the east shores of Llyn Edno before climbing to a cairn on the north side of the Ysgafell Wen ridge. From here you can look down the length of the Yr Arddu ridge.

Just south of this you come to the north top beyond which there is a drop to the head of the Lledr Valley. The ridge here is ill defined in places, and punctuated by numerous rock knolls. The path has developed close to the posts of the old parish fence rather than the more modern and intact one. It heads SSW past the most westerly of three crag-ringed lakes known collectively as Llynnau'r Cwn (the dog lakes). After passing the lakes the path comes to the south top, where another pile of stones marks the highest point of the ridge.

Opposite: Moel Meirch seen from Yr Arddu ridge.

Ysgafell Wen, the white brow, can be seen from both Nantgwynant and the Lledr Valley as a long, crag-serrated ridge. In fact, the ridge divides beyond the south top. One arm continues south-west to Cnicht, the other south-east to Moel Druman and Allt Fawr. The south top also sends out a craggy spur which, along with the main ridge, encloses a wild cwm of tussocky moor grass, crag and heather. Here, the Afon Lledr is born as a mere trickle, before surging its way through Dolwyddelan to Betws y Coed.

Ysgafell Wen is well known for its mountain tarns. There are numerous small pools on the ridge itself, but added to these are the three rushy, rockbound pools known as Llynnau'r Cwm (the dog lakes) and Llyn Edno, an L-shaped tarn set beautifully among rocky bluffs and heather. Further afield on the lower Nantgwynant slopes there's Llyn Llagi, a beautiful circular sheet of water, backed up by sheer cliffs and fed by a spout-like waterfall which has been fed by Llyn yr Adar, a huge lake on a high grassy shelf beneath Ysgafell Wen. An island in the middle of Llyn yr Adar is often colonized by hundreds of cackling gulls.

While the Nantgwynant side of the mountain is complex and exquisitely embellished with woodland, high meadow and exciting crags, the Lledr side is untamed, spacious and strangely dramatic. The slopes that rise to the northernmost top are really quite steep but there are no paths to invite you to the top, just tussocks and heather which catch the sunlight beautifully but have a penchant for untying your bootlaces and tangling around your ankles.

Opposite: One of the three Llynau'r Cwm (lakes) on Ysgafell Wen's summit ridge, with Snowdon behind.
Below: Ysgafell Wen and Yr Arddu seen across the upper Lledr Valley.

Route MSN12

Nantgwynant and Llyn Llagi

Scenically one of the most beautiful walks in the region

Start: Britannia car park, Nantgwynant (GR: SH 628507)

Distance: 3¼ miles/6km

Height gain: 2200ft/670m

Time: 2–2½ hours

From the north end of the car park, follow Plas Gwynant's tarmac drive before taking the left fork, a stony track through the woodlands north of the main buildings. A footpath waymarker points the way. A delightful path, cushioned by fallen rhododendron leaves, descends through woodland, across the foaming Afon Llynedno and out on to the narrow tarmac Nantmor Lane.

Turn left along the lane to the converted chapel of Blaen Nant (GR 635490), where a path descends from the left side of the road to pass a small cottage before crossing a stream. The whitewashed Llwynyrhwch farm, delightfully situated among oak and rhododendron, lies ahead. Go over the stile and pass in front of the farmhouse before turning right at the waymarker just beyond. From here the path goes over a stile, climbs rock outcrops and tucks beneath oak woods to continue through a complex but beautiful landscape of pasture, drystone walls and foaming cataracts flowing through broad-leaved copses.

As the path passes beneath Craig Wen, watch out for a left fork, which rakes up firmer grassy slopes rather than following the marshy track to Llyn Llagi's shore. When you

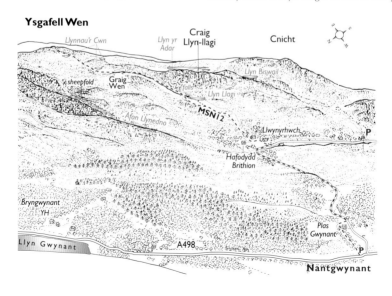

see it first the circular tarn is completely over-shadowed by the spectacular near-vertical cliffs that tower from its eastern edge. The expanse of rock is briefly interrupted by a cascade fed by the Llyn yr Adar, 180m above.

The path climbs past an old quarry slag heap and into a grassy corridor between crags and to the left of Craig Llyn-llagi's cliffs. At a cairn ignore the faint path on the right but continue through a little rocky hollow straight ahead. The narrow path passes to the left of two of the three Dog Lakes (Llynnau'r Cwn). From the second it's a short clamber to get to the ridge fence. Here you turn left past another small pool. After a slight curve to the left, the path comes upon the higher south top and its pile of stones.

Other route options

There's a variation of Route MSN12 taking in Llyn yr Adar (turn right on the marked footpath above Llyn Llagi). On reaching the col above Llyn yr Adar turn left (north-east) to climb to the south top.

Below: The complex hill slopes that lead from Bwlch Rhosydd and its quarries to Ysgafell Wen, which lies on the skyline to the left.

RIDGE ROUTES

Moel Meirch

Distance: 1¼ miles/2.8km
Height gain: 330ft/100m
Time: 1 hour

This is a straightforward route along an undulating rocky summit ridge high above the cwm of the Afon Lledr. Llynnau'r Cwn, the dog lakes, come into view in their respective rocky hollows then, beyond the north top, there's a descent down to the east shore of Llyn Edno. Leave the fence-side ridge path for a left fork path winding and climbing over slopes of bilberry and crag to reach the rocky summit of Moel Meirch.

Moel Druman/Allt Fawr

Distance: 1¼ miles/1.9km
Height gain: 330ft/ 100m
Time: ¾ hour

Descend by the fence from the south summit skirting the east shore of Llyn Terfyn and close to Llyn Coch before making the short climb to Moel Druman. The narrow path continues across rough moor and threads through the gap between the huge Llyn Conglog and a small unnamed pool. Allt Fawr lies ahead now and the fence that has been a ridge fence this far now climbs its flanks. Go over a ladder stile in the fence and climb half-left (ESE) to the summit.

Cnicht

Distance: 1¼ miles/2.7km
Height gain: 460ft/ 140m
Time: 1 hour

From the south summit head south-west on a trackless course across a vague ridge heading towards Cnicht. Down below you to the right will be a large lake, Llyn yr Adar, lying in a marshy hollow – it's easily recognised by the rocky island in the middle. On reaching a cairn at a shallow col, ignore the descending paths on the left and right but climb directly ahead on a reasonably well-defined path to the rocky bluffs marking the start of the Cnicht ridge. Three small summits later, the path reaches the top.

Above: Llyn Llagi and the cliffs of Craig Llyn-llagi.

Craig Llyn-llagi is the Pavey Ark of Snowdonia: it's a fine wall of crag above a beautifully sited mountain tarn. Many walkers will have seen the dark shadow of the cliffs and cwm from distant Snowdon, but the scene will probably have passed from their memories as their eyes moved on to the spectacles of steam trains, hungry gulls and the misty blue hills of the southern horizon. The fact that few walkers will have heard of this splendid peak is because hardly anybody ventures far off the tracks in the Nantgwynant Hills – they're all on Cnicht or Moel Siabod.

From the east, Craig Llyn-llagi is just a low jagged crest jutting out from the shores of Llyn yr Adar. But it really does look the business from the west – here you get a full frontal view of those cliffs and the cascade plummeting down one of the gulleys.

There are no paths to Craig Llyn-llagi and there are no cairns for those who like to 'touch the top' before ticking their list. However, when you're sitting on the summit rocks or peering down one of the cliff face's awesome gulleys to Llyn Llagi below, you still get that top-of-the-world feeling.

Route MSN13

Nantgwynant and Llyn Llagi

A scenically stunning walk to a seldom-trodden peak

Start: Gelli-iago car park, Nantmor Road above Nantgwynant (GR: SH 632484)

Distance: 2¼ miles/3.6km

Height gain: 1440ft/440m

Time: 1½ hours

From the car park turn right along the Nantmor Road past the old quarries to reach the whitewashed cottage of Blaen Nant (GR 635490). Turn right here on a signed path descending to a small cottage and crossing a small stream before climbing towards Llwynyrhwch farm. Go over the stile and pass in front of the farmhouse and turn right at the waymarker just beyond.

From here the path goes over a stile, climbs

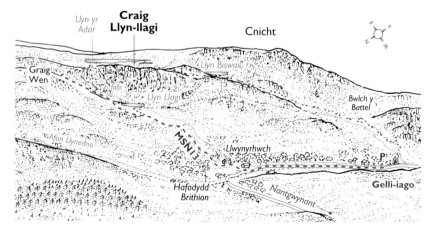

rock outcrops and tucks beneath oak woods. A couple of fine whitewater streams come tumbling down the hillsides hereabouts, and although there are a few marshy places, often handily placed stepping stones have been provided. The shadowy crags above Llyn Llagi are visible on the skyline but the hillscapes are dominated at this stage by the powerfully shaped dome of Craig Wen, the white crag.

As the path passes beneath Craig Wen, watch out for a left fork, which rakes up firmer grass slopes rather than following the marshy track to Llyn Llagi's shore. The path climbs past an old quarry slag heap and into a grassy corridor between crags and to the left of Craig Llyn-llagi's cliffs.

Halfway up the corridor, a cairn marks the divergence of the right of way shown on the map. The course of the right of way is not obvious at first but if you look west up the bouldery slopes you should be able to pick up a narrow path about 100m further on. The path gains confidence and takes the route up the shoulder of the hill. The views of Snowdon from here are quite spectacular.

The path makes the ridge and soon Llyn yr Adar appears in the view ahead – it's a huge tarn with an island and two attendant pools on its nearside. Don't follow the path traversing marshy ground to the left of the lake, but instead turn right to cross its outflow stream before climbing the grass and crag slopes which soon take you to the rocks that form the top of the cliffs above Llyn Llagi. Glimpses down to the lake are provided by the odd gully.

It's a magical top, hardly ever walked. Cnicht is monarch of the southern panorama while Snowdon rules in the north.

Below: On the summit of Craig Llyn-llagi.

Other route options

The obvious one starts at Gelli-iago and follows the stream towards Bwlch y Battel. The main path should be left at GR 638474, where the climb starts right over a patch of bouldery terrain and away from the stream. Just stay parallel to the river and you'll locate a path, which soon crosses marshy grassland to a ladder stile.

Follow the outflow of Llyn Biswail, which tumbles down a hollow between two craggy spurs, to the tarn, follow the south-east shores, then head north across the left shoulder of Foel Boethwel, the rocky knoll overlooking the north shore. Craig Llyn-llagi is the serrated rocky ridge lying due north, an easy clamber over boulder and grass. The huge tarn of Llyn yr Adar will appear on the right in a wide grassy bowl.

RIDGE ROUTES

Ysgafell Wen

Distance: 1¼ miles/2km
Height gain: 410ft/125m
Time: ¼ hour

There are no paths but the route in clear conditions presents no problems. First, head north-east along Craig Llyn-llagi's crest before descending to cross the outflow of Llyn yr Adar. Arc right around the perimeter of the tarn's marshy hollow.

For a direct route to the north top, climb north-eastwards by the feeder stream. You should meet the most southerly of the Llynnau'r Cwn, the dog lakes. Maintain direction among the crags to the most easterly of these three tarns, from where it is a short climb to the main ridge and Ysgafell Wen's north top. For the highest south top, just head south by the ridge fence.

For a direct route to the south top continue along the north side of Llyn yr Adar. Take the very faint left fork at GR 657481. This climbs to the ridge at Llyn Terfyn. Climb left by the fence to the cairned south top.

Cnicht

Distance: 1¼ miles/2.7km
Height gain: 475ft/145m
Time: 1 hour

Initially there's no path. Head north-east along Craig Llyn-llagi's crest before descending to cross the outflow of Llyn yr Adar. Turn right on meeting the faint path on the far bank. The path skirts the marshy ground on the north side of Llyn yr Adar before climbing to a cairn on a low col beyond. Turn right (SW) on the grassy ridge going over successive rock knolls until you come to Cnicht's summit.

MOEL DRUMAN

ALLT FAWR

Often referred to as a 2000-footer in its own right, Moel Druman is little more than a bump in the ridge – its name, which means the bare hill of the ridge, tells you that. While it has pleasing craggy north slopes above an unnamed cwm, it's little more than a knuckle at the end of Allt Fawr.

Like Ysgafell Wen, Moel Druman will be remembered for its high lakes. There's one on the north-west side, Llyn Coch, and several to the south-east, the largest being Llyn Conglog. The ridge is wild and windswept but has a wire fence running along its length. To the south, extremely complex slopes with tiered rock steps and many more miners' reservoirs lead down to Bwlch y Rhosydd, a large shelf of quarried land separating the slate valleys of Cwm Croesor and Cwmorthin.

Allt Fawr, the big slope, is the highest summit of a craggy ridge curving around the deserted cwm at the head of the Lledr Valley. It's the monarch of the Crimea peaks.

Unfortunately, when viewed from Blaenau Ffestiniog and the Crimea Pass, the mountain is horribly disfigured by the old Oakeley slate quarries on its eastern slopes. But don't be put off: the scars and slag heaps are soon left behind for seemingly remote ridges. The mining scars and relics seen in the higher cwms are slowly mouldering into the mountainsides and passing into history.

When seen from Upper Cwmorthin, Allt Fawr shows its pedigree, for that big slope is magnificently precipitous. With diagonal ribs of rock and scree flecked with dark heather, it flows down in graceful arcs to the shores of the valley's huge lake.

Being so close to the more famous Moelwyn peaks and Cnicht, Allt Fawr is often an afterthought on the walker's itinerary, a late visit after Cnicht and Moelwyn Mawr. To do justice to this fine peak, you should do it first, probably starting from the Crimea Pass and taking in the splendid views of Llyn Iwerddon and the high eastern face. To complete the wild and desolate theme the whole of the upper cwm of the Lledr could be rounded on Ysgafell Wen and Yr Arddu. A good track wandering through the complex terrain of hills eases the route back to the Crimea Pass.

Route MSN14
The Crimea Pass
Rising above the crumbling world of slate
Start: Crimea Pass car park (GR: SH 702489)
Distance: 2¾ miles/4.4km
Height gain: 1475ft/450m
Time: 1½ hours

Climb the road to the top of the pass before going over a ladder stile on the right, from where a wide cart track doubles back northwards. Below, bleak moorland descends to the Lledr Valley, overshadowed by the cone of Moel Siabod. As the grassy ridge to the left descends to track level (before the first sharp U-turn), double back WSW.

It's all pathless in these early stages, but as you climb out of a hollow beneath some crags you'll come to a ladder stile in a fence (GR 696486). Now you look down on Llyn Ffridd-y-bwlch, a dismal little tarn backed up by the even more dismal wastelands of slate that surround Blaenau Ffestiniog.

Go over the stile and turn right to follow a faint path alongside the fence and westwards up grassy slopes. The eye seeks solace from all the awful slag heaps and soon finds it in the form of a lonely lake, Llyn Dyrnogydd. Actually, there's something industrial hidden beneath your feet: if you put your ear to the ground you may hear a rumble. It's the railway, which burrows two miles into the hillsides hereabouts.

Left: The view from Allt Fawr to
Llyn Iwerddon.

271

The fence you've been following descends to the lake, while the path continues uphill to a pleasing rocky ridge. Then there's another lake, Llyn Iwerddon – it's nicer but you still have to look at the slate lower down. But in the view ahead, looking imposing and well-structured, is Allt Fawr. There's a little bit of descent to be made before tackling those slopes.

The path gets shy on its way up those steep slopes, often hiding behind ribs of rock. But it's easy to thread your way through the bluffs to find the summit. Looking back along the ridge, Llyn Iwerddon looks much more impressive now, sheltering beneath the splintered cliffs. In the opposite direction, Cnicht and the big Moelwynion dominate the scene, rising high above the old quarry barracks of Cwmorthin and Rhosydd.

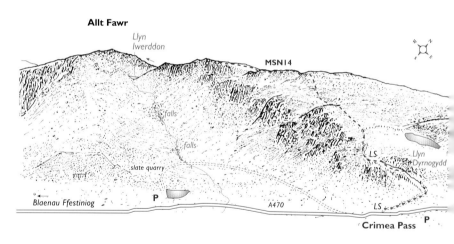

Opposite: Allt Fawr across Cwmorthin.

Route MSN15

Cwmorthin and Rhosydd

Lofty windswept lakes and a dramatic slate
cwm highlight a fascinating route

Start: Car park above Tanygrisiau, beginning
of Cwmorthin track (GR: SH 683454)

Distance: 3¼ miles/6km

Height gain: 1770ft/540m

Time: 2 hours

The route begins on a stony track tracing
the east bank of the Afon Cwmorthin. Cross
the river on a slab bridge beneath the old
Cwmorthin barracks and just short of the
reservoir dam. A quarry track now continues
past a ruined chapel to the head of the cwm,
where it swings left to climb to Bwlch
Rhosydd and its slate mines. Look out for a
sketchy track climbing up slopes to the right.
Cairned in places, this leads past the cliffs of
Clogwyn Brith and the little lake beneath.

On reaching the concrete dam of Llyn
Cwm-corsiog, leave the path and climb right
(trackless) on a craggy arm with views down
tremendous slabbed slopes, which plunge
down to Cwmorthin. Note how majestic the
pointed peak of Moel-yr-hydd looks from
here.

The route comes to a marshy plateau
where Llyn Conglog stretches out to the little
peak of Moel Druman. Not far beyond it the
route comes to a fence leading up the north
flank of Allt Fawr. Go over a ladder stile in the
fence before climbing ESE up grass slopes to
the summit.

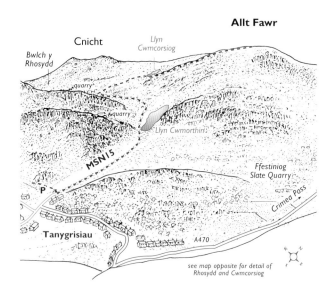

Allt Fawr

Cnicht

Llyn Cwmcorsiog

Bwlch y Rhosydd

quarry

quarry

Llyn Cwmorthin

MSN15

Ffestiniog Slate Quarry

P

Crimea Pass

Tanygrisiau

A470

see map opposite for detail of
Rhosydd and Cwmcorsiog

Other route options

It's perfectly feasible to climb Allt Fawr from Croesor by way of Bwlch y Rhosydd where Route MSN13 would continue to the summit, but most other routes would be contrived. One very rough alternative would be to start at Blaenau Dolwyddelan and follow the winding flinted track to the east of the Afon Lledr from the north end of the railway tunnel to the sharp bend by the air shaft (GR 691494) before climbing south (pathless) to the Moel Dyrnogydd ridge, joining Route MSN12 to the summit.

RIDGE ROUTE

Moel Druman/Ysgafell Wen

Distance: 1¼ miles/1.9km
Height gain: 330ft/100m
Time: ¼ hour

A recently constructed electric fence cuts across the ridge west of the summit. But descend west (half-right) to a ladder stile in the fence. The lovely green path that you see alongside the fence turns out to be unfit to walk on.

A sheep track alongside traverses rough moor. It squeezes into the gap between the huge Llyn Conglog and a small unnamed pool before tackling the rocky knoll that is Moel Druman. A fence acts as a guide to Llyn Coch, where it turns left and ceases to be of use. From here the remains of the old fence take the route past Llyn Terfyn and up a bouldery route to the south top of Ysgafell Wen.

Allt Fawr

Llyn Conglog
Cwmorthin
Foel Ddu
Llyn Cwmcorsiog
MSN 19 path to Cnicht
MSN15 from Tanygrisiau
quarry
Barracks
MSN15
Bwlch y Rhosydd

Cnicht, which means the knight, has been called the Matterhorn of Wales. Seen from the Glaslyn valley, where it exhibits an impressive pyramid of rock, there seems some justification.

Spellbound by this bold façade, nearly all walkers choose to climb Cnicht from Croesor, a small village on the low hillside just above the Glaslyn Estuary. It's a pretty walk, with the pyramid nearly always in view. However, that bold suit of armour is merely a front, for when the walker gets to the top he or she is presented with a long, undulating ridge.

Cnicht is one of the most enjoyable hills in Snowdonia. The rocky scramble up its nose is exciting though not frightening, with the views down the precipices to the cavernous Cwm Croesor adding spice to the mix of peak and pasture. Once you're up on the summit you can relax. It's a pleasing ridge, with grass interspersed with rocky knolls. All around there are sapphire tarns sparkling in the hollows and cwms, and you can stroll to wherever takes your fancy – there are so many options in the complex system of ridges and peaks.

Cnicht has two main summits and a third minor rocky knoll, but the one at the Croesor end is the highest. Of those tarns, Llyn Biswail is the prettiest, lying in a verdant shallow basin rimmed with shattered rock outcrops. Further distant is Llyn yr Adar, the lake of the birds – and the cries of its resident gulls may well be echoing in the breeze. You may spot grass of Parnassus in the acidic soils of the ridge's marshy places, like those surrounding some of the lakes. The plant has heart-shaped leaves and solitary flowers at the end of a longish stem. Many of the lakes are breeding grounds for the now not-so-common sandpiper, a small wading bird with sandy brown head and wings and a white throat.

On the north-west side of the mountain, high above Nantgwynant at Gelli-iago, a fast-flowing whitewater stream tumbles down a rocky gorge, lined with rowan. It's the ideal way to sneak up on the knight to see him in his true colours. What you'll find is a splendid, still shapely scree-scraped craggy ridge, a connoisseurs' hill where the lack of people allows opportunities for quiet contemplation and for appreciation of more subtle beauty. But then you're rudely confronted with that gob-smacking view down the precipices of Cwm Croesor!

Opposite: Cnicht seen across the huge hollow of Cwm Croesor.

Route MSN16
Llyn Llagi

A long but very beautiful route
Start: Nantgwynant car park
  (GR: SH 628507)
Distance: 4 miles/7km
Height gain: 2300ft/700m
Time: 2½ hours

From the north end of the car park, follow Plas Gwynant's tarmac drive before taking the left fork, a stony track through the woodlands north of the main buildings. A footpath waymarker points the way down a delightful path through rhododendron bushes and woodland, to cross the Afon Llynedno on a footbridge before coming to the narrow tarmac Nantmor Lane.

Turn left along the lane and climb with it around one sharp right-hand bend, then for a further half-mile/800m to the converted chapel of Blaen Nant. Here, take the path on the left, descending to a small cottage and crossing a small stream before climbing towards Llwynyrhwch farm. Go over the stile and pass in front of the farmhouse before turning right at the waymarker just beyond. From here the path goes over a stile, climbs

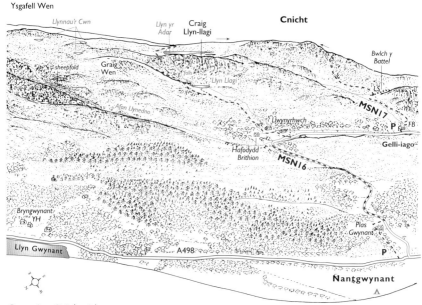

Opposite: Cnicht ridge.

rock outcrops and tucks beneath oakwoods. The well-defined path continues eastwards past more rock outcrops and rough pasture. The going becomes more marshy as the path approaches Llyn Llagi, a circular tarn completely overshadowed by the sullen vertical cliffs that tower from its eastern edge and by a cascade fed by the waters of Llyn yr Adar, which lies some 600ft/180m above. Make sure you take the faint left fork raking up the firmer ground rather than staying on the level path through marshy terrain – this would lead to the lake shore.

The path climbs to the left of the cliffs, just beyond a stream crossing, at a point marked by a cairn. Faint at first, it turns to the south, rising on a bouldery course to the ridge before veering south-west to reach the shores of Llyn yr Adar. The large lake is rounded on its east side, traversing marshy grassland before climbing to the col between Ysgafell Wen and Cnicht (GR 657477). Here you should turn right (south-west) along an undulating but clear ridge path to the summit of Cnicht.

Route MSN17
Gelli-iago and Bwlch y Battel

Quiet but very pleasant route taking in a splendid outlying summit

Start: Roadside car park, Gelli-iago, Nantmor Road (GR: SH 632484)
Distance: 2½ miles/4km
Height gain: 2100ft/640m
Time: 1½ hours

From the roadside car park on the Nantmor Road, turn left along the track to the cottage of Gelli-iago. Go through the gate to pass to the left of the cottage, then turn right beyond another gate on to a footbridge across the stream. A stony path now winds up the hillside while the stream on the left tumbles down through rocks studded with rowan, hawthorn and heather. Cnicht's rocky sides soon come into view ahead as you traverse wet moorland.

On reaching a ladder stile in the wild pass of Bwlch y Battel, leave the path and veer left beneath the broken ridge towards a clear scree run on Cnicht's flanks. A faint path develops and leads to the bottom of the scree run, which then leads on to the main Cnicht ridge. Turn left on a narrow path scrambling up the mountain's final rocky slopes. Although exhilarating, the route is never exposed.

Opposite: Cnicht from above Gelli-iago.

Route MSN18
Croesor and the South-West Ridge
The classic and most popular route
Start: Croesor (GR: SH 632447)
Distance: 2 miles/3km
Height gain: 1770ft/540m
Time: 1½ hours

From the car park, follow the village road north-east past the old chapel to its terminus. Continue along an undulating stony track through woodland to a junction on open hillsides where you turn right. A waymarker highlights a right turn at a path junction. Over the next stile the path climbs north-east, with Cnicht in full view ahead. At first the route stays to the north (left side) of the ridge's crest, but eventually it takes a peep over the Cwm Croesor side where Moelwyn Mawr looks particularly regal.

The route soon steepens and tackles that final rocky pyramid in an exhilarating but easy scramble to the summit. Although you're always aware of the great rock and scree slopes plunging into Cwm Croesor, as on the previous Route MSN17 the path never feels too exposed.

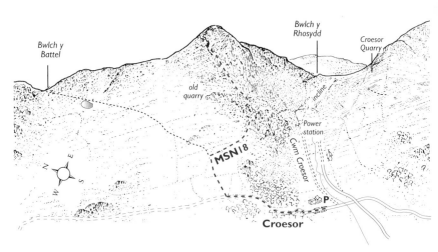

Opposite: Climbing Cnicht's south-west ridge above Croesor.

Route MSN19

Tanygrisiau and Cwmorthin

A fascinating route through industrial history

Start: Tanygrisiau – small car park just off the
Stwlan Dam road (GR: SH 683453)

Distance: 3¼ miles (6km)

Height gain: 1610ft/490m

Time: 2 hours

Turn right out of the car park then left across
the road bridge over the Afon Cwmorthin
before turning left on the other side to follow
a lane climbing parallel to the river. Where
the lane ends, continue along a stony quarry
road, climbing to the shores of Llyn Cwmorthin.

Cross a slate bridge spanning the river to
pass beneath Cwmorthin Barracks and continue past a derelict chapel and its gaunt surrounding pine trees towards the end of the
cwm. Here the track arcs left to climb past
more quarry buildings and mountains of slag
to reach the high pass of Bwlch y Rhosydd,
where a vast shelf of high land is scattered
with the remains of slate quarries and mines.

Opposite the main quarry barracks you
should spot a faint path climbing the hillside
to the right. This tucks under the cliffs of Clogwyn y Brith and its small tarn and passes Llyn
Cwm-corsiog before continuing over a series
of tiered crags to arrive at the cairned col
overlooking Llyn yr Adar. Turn left here to
climb steadily along a long grassy ridge to
Cnicht's summit.

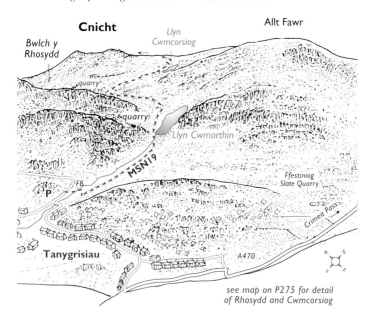

see map on P275 for detail
of Rhosydd and Cwmcorsiog

Other route options

From Cwm Croesor it is possible to take the slanting path on the low sides of Cnicht's southern face to Llyn Cwm-y-foel before tackling the steep south face in a northerly direction or alternatively by following the reservoir's feeder stream to the col used by route MSN19. A splendid route from Bwlch-gwernog (GR 597462) near Nantmor uses an old Roman road, Sarn Helen, which winds along the plateau south of Yr Arddu to join the main Croesor route (Route MSN18) at GR 628452.

RIDGE ROUTES

Ysgafell Wen

Distance: 1¼ miles/2.7km
Height gain: 430ft/ 130m
Time: 1 hour

Head north-east along the grassy ridge down to the shallow col overlooking Llyn yr Adar. Ignoring paths descending left and right maintain your direction up craggy slopes to the ridge fence on Ysgafell Wen's south top.

Below: Cwmorthin Barracks.

CERRIG-Y-MYLLT AND YR ARDDU (NANTMOR)

The Cerrig-y-myllt–Yr Arddu ridge comprises a complex of rocky hummocks which are rhyolitic tuffs capping an area of dolerite sills. The former strata are quite often heather-clad; the latter grassy. Yr Arddu was in fact the centre of a minor volcanic eruption, which occurred beneath the sea. Looking at the ground between the summit and Cerrig-y-myllt you may spot the Yr Arddu syncline, a downfolding of the local rocks that continues to the little peak of Y Castell on the far side of Bwlch y Battel.

Cerrig-y-myllt, which has the unfortunate meaning of the stone of the castrated ram (goodness knows what locals used to get up to here!), is the highest summit, although it's not named on current maps. It's dome-shaped with rounded terraces of pale crag, protruding from its carpets of heather.

Yr Arddu, which means the darkness, lies to the south. Its summit is topped with a small spiky cairn and overlooks some strange, layer-cake, cement-grey dolerite rock knolls, which look as if they belong to Arizona or Utah rather than Gwynedd.

The extremely rugged terrain offers much to the curious walker who has strayed off the well-trodden routes, for here is a wonderland highlighted by lazy pools which are often perfectly calm and reflecting the sky and the crags like precious sparkling gemstones. The views of both Snowdon and Cnicht would be reward in itself, but there's so much more to these little peaks. You may even see an osprey scouring the crags, as indeed I did.

Opposite: Cerrig-y-myllt as seen from Cnicht. Here is fascinating mountainside in miniature, studded with crags, sapphire-like tarns and carpeted with lush heather.

Route MSN20

Cerrig-y-myllt, Gelli-iago and Bwlch y Battel

*Quiet but very pleasant route taking in a
splendid outlying summit*

Start: Roadside car park, Gelli-iago,
Nantmor Road (GR: SH 632484)

Distance: 1½ miles/2.6km

Height gain: 1020ft/310m

Time: 1–1¼ hours

From the roadside car park on the Nantmor
Road turn left along the track to the cottage of
Gelli-iago. Go through the gate to pass to the
left of the cottage, then turn right beyond
another gate on to a footbridge across the
stream. A stony path now winds up the hillside. The stream on the left tumbles down
through rocks studded with rowan, hawthorn
and heather.

Cnicht's rocky sides soon come into view
ahead as the path, bouldery in places, crosses
the wet moors. Once over a ladder stile in the
wild pass of Bwlch y Battel, climb half-right
(west), slanting away from a tall drystone wall
and up grassy slopes towards the crags forming the northern ridge of Cerrig-y-myllt.

Eventually sheep-tracks preceding those
crags take the route up a grassy hollow that
leads to the twin lakes of Llynnau Cerrig-y-
myllt. A clear but narrow path threads
between the lakes and winds around the right
side of a rock bluff before trending left and
descending slightly to another grassy hollow.
Turn right (SSW) and follow this before
turning right again (NW) to climb steadily
through a grassy weakness in the crags. On
reaching the ridge turn left along narrow
tracks over rocks and heather to reach Cerrig-
y-myllt's summit.

Cerrig-y-myllt

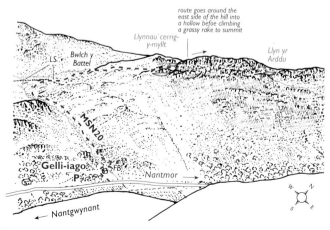

route goes around the
east side of the hill into
a hollow befoe climbing
a grassy rake to summit

Llynnau cerrig-
y-myllt

Llyn yr
Arddu

Bwlch y
Battel

LS

MSN20

Gelli-iago

P   FB

Nantmor

Nantgwynant

*Opposite: Cerrig-y-
myllt and one of its
fine lakes.*

Route MSN21

Yr Arddu from Coed Caeddafydd

A complex and stiff climb but worth it for the views alone

Start: Lay-by car park, Nantmor Road
  (GR: SH 620468)

Distance: 1 mile/1.5km

Height gain: 1050ft/320m

Time: 1 hour

Note: Due to problems of navigation, this route is totally unsuitable when mist and low cloud prevail

---

Turn right along the road, then right again on a signed footpath through a rough enclosed field. The path, not clear underfoot, rounds the left side of a patch of bracken and a crumbling drystone top wall. Beyond this a stony path develops, angling right through woodland.

The steep path goes through a gate at the top edge of the woods, then runs roughly parallel to conifer plantations on the right. Unlike the right of way marked on the map, it does not enter the woods but fades into the marshy ground near the top corner of the plantation. Here you angle right through a gap in a wall, follow a fence for a few paces, then go through another gap in the intake wall. The course of the path on the map doesn't exist and the crags ahead are interspersed with thick heather and bracken.

The best way forward is to climb alongside the forest's top edge. On reaching the highest point of this course, turn left to climb on a narrow and very faint path through the heather. This fades for a while but by maintaining direction up slopes of heather and crag you should pick up another narrow path angling right before veering half-left to climb up a gulley. In the upper stages you find your-

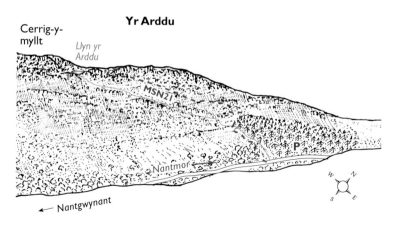

Cerrig-y-myllt

Yr Arddu

Llyn yr Arddu

MSN21

P

Nantmor

← Nantgwynant

self looking across the hollow cut by the out-flow stream of Llyn Arddu. The path disappears again on the high slopes but the going gets a little easier, and the view back to Moel Hebog, the Nantlle Ridge and Snowdon offers more than adequate compensation.

On reaching the ridge, just north-east of Yr Arddu's summit, wonderful scenes of Cnicht and the Moelwynion come into view across a vast desert of heather and ribs of crag. A path of sorts cuts across a marshy grassed area and skirts the high south-west side of Yr Arddu's ridge. As height is gained the beautiful Llyn Arddu comes into view to the north.

Climb right (pathless) where the heather becomes short and the slopes shallow. The summit will be very close and highlighted by a spiky cairn.

Other route options

The track leading from Bwlchgwernog (GR 612453) or from Croesor village could be used to reach the track junction at GR 628 451. The route would then climb past the small lake to Bwlch y Battel where Route MSN21 leads up grass slopes, then over heather and crag to the summit of Cerrig-y-myllt. For Yr Arddu, leave the bridleway track just beyond the rock knoll at GR 636464 and climb to the crags overlooking Llyn Arddu. Turn left to round the tarn on high ground along the near shores before climbing left to the summit.

Below: Climbing Yr Arddu from Nantmor.

RIDGE ROUTES

Yr Arddu to Cerrig-y-myllt

Distance: ¾ mile/1.2km
Height gain: 330ft/100m
Time: ½–¾ hour

Descend a short distance eastwards from the summit on short heather to easier grass-and-heather terrain, then head directly north-east for Llyn Arddu. On nearing the lake veer right on to higher ground to avoid the marshy surrounds. Sheep-paths lead to a slight depression occupied by tiny marsh-surrounded pool (GR 631466).

After crossing this depression well to the left of the pool, descend left before climbing a grassy corridor between rocky crags. The high one to the left is Cerrig-y-myllt. A shepherds' path soon develops. Follow it to its high point. A faint and narrow path climbs left before disappearing among the crags, but it's easy to pick your way around ribs of rock to reach the summit.

Cerrig-y-myllt to Cnicht

Distance: 1 mile/1.8km
Height gain: 1020ft/310m
Time: 40–50 minutes

Descend north-west from the summit down the rocky ridge until a grassy corridor takes the route left to a shepherds' track descending left towards the shores of Llynnau Cerrig-y-myllt's more easterly lake. On nearing the shoreline the path veers left to climb around a rocky knoll to pass between the two lakes and over a low rocky outcrop. A fading path continues down a grassy hollow to a tall dry-stone wall, then right alongside the wall to a ladder stile at Bwlch y Battel, where the Croesor–Gelli-iago path crosses.

Don't go over the stile but instead climb beneath the broken ridge ahead and towards a clear scree run on Cnicht's flanks. A faint path develops and leads to the bottom of the scree run, which then leads on to the main Cnicht ridge. Turn left, following the path scrambling up the mountain's final rocky slopes.

The highest summit in a range of low hills rising from the east side of Beddgelert, Moel Dyniewyd is protected on the south and east sides by a wall of cliffs that glare across the wooded valley of Nantmor. Although the west side of the range around Bwlch y Sygun is often crowded with walkers, most are content to omit Moel Dyniewyd – all the better for those who like the peaks to themselves. A pair of ospreys has settled in the valley below and can often be seen in the skies. It is to be hoped that they will breed successfully, for this is the only pair in Wales.

Besides the previously mentioned cliffs the vegetation of forest, crag and thick heather makes exploration from Nantmor difficult and there are only two access points: one near Buarthau, the other a short way south. Both are reached using the footpath from the picnic site at Coed Caeddafydd.

Below: The summit of Moel Dyniewyd with Snowdon behind.

Route MSN22
Llyn Dinas

A splendid outlying summit

Start: Lay-by car park, Llyn Dinas
    (GR: SH 613494)
Distance: 1½ miles/2.5km
Height gain: 1115ft/340m
Time: ¾–1 hour

Follow the footpath on the lake side of the road along the shore of the lake before turning left to cross the footbridge spanning the Afon Glaslyn. A left turn along the far bank returns the route to the lake shore, but this path is abandoned for one climbing hill slopes to the right.

The path winds up a heathery hollow to reach the old mine levels at Grib Ddu, where the path divides. Turn left here to reach a ladder stile over a fence. Don't cross but follow a narrow path on the left that roughly follows the line of the fence. Peaty in places, stony in others, the path climbs up heather-cloaked, craggy hillside to an unnamed peak (315m spot height on Explorer maps) before dropping slightly to a shallow depression occupied by a small tarn.

The path scrambles up steep rocky slopes, by the fence at first. Take care, for the fence has eye-level barbed wire (why landowners do such things I don't know, for no sheep is going to high-jump a tall wire fence scaling a 30-degree slope). Go over the ladder stile in the fence at GR 611478 and continue on a narrow path. There's a short scramble over rock just a few paces from the summit.

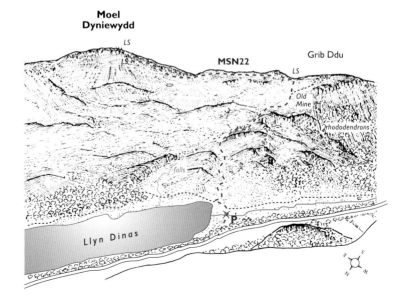

Other route options

Unfortunately, as stated above, there are only two usable access points from the Nantmor Valley. Both are reached using the footpath from the picnic site at Coed Caeddafydd. The second is the best option, one with no walls to scale which leaves the footpath at GR 621473 before climbing through forest. It continues the climb over hillsides of rock and bracken, past a sheepfold and through a weakness in the fringe of cliffs, where the course of a stream takes you to a small lake. Here it's an easy climb to the ridge fence between Moel Dyniewyd and Mynydd Llyndi. Turn left for the summit.

RIDGE ROUTES

Mynydd Sygun

Distance: 1⅓ miles/2.2km
Height gain: 280ft/85m
Time: ¾ hour

Descend north-westwards by the fence to a shallow depression by a small lake. Over the next rise and across a sea of heather the narrow path meets a wider one by a ladder stile. Don't cross it, but follow the wide path northwards to a three-way junction by the rocks of Crib Ddu. Follow the path on the left signed to Beddgelert and Sygun, and go over another ladder stile in a fence.

After negotiating a high rock-step with good footholds, the route winds down Bwlch y Sygun on a stony path to a grassy hollow before coming to the Nantgwynant edge. The path now heads south-west along the Nant-gwynant side of the ridge. Take the next left fork path to a large cairn back on the ridge crest (GR 600479). Now follow a narrower path along the craggy crest to reach the cairned top of Mynydd Sygun.

Overleaf: The rugged little peak of Moel Dyniewyd seen across Nantmor.

Beddgelert's very own mountain is steep-sided, craggy and covered with rhododendrons, whose vivid pink blooms create a bizarre blaze of colour in early summer.

Although lacking in height, Mynydd Sygun's mountainscapes are impressive, with rocky knolls overlooking desolate grassy hollows and cwms. The hillsides above Nantmor featured in the famous Ingrid Bergman film, *The Inn of the Sixth Happiness,* the story of London-born missionary Gladys Aylward, who went to northern China in 1930–49. For the same film the village of Yangcheng was reconstructed in Cwm Bychan. Cwm Bychan today is rather forlorn, a grassy hollow threading between splintered, craggy moun-

tainsides patched with heather, boulder and bracken. There's a line of rusting gantries, part of an old aerial ropeway built to carry copper ore down to a crushing mill. Mining had taken place hereabouts since Roman times, but after World War I the extraction became uneconomical and in 1922 the mines closed.

The south ridge of Mynydd Sygun declines to Pont Aberglaslyn and the mountain's most famous feature, the sheer cliffs that form one side of the Aberglaslyn Pass. Here, the Afon Glaslyn is white and furious, forging its way over a bed of huge boulders. Before the building of William Madock's embankment in 1811, it would have flowed through a beautiful estuary out to the sea and Nantmor, the sea stream, meant what it said on the signpost.

Opposite: On Bwlch Sygun.
Below: Grib Ddu on the Mynydd Sygun ridge.

Route MSN23
Cwm Bychan

A pleasant route past industrial relics
Start: Pont Aberglaslyn car park
  (GR: SH 597462)
Distance: 1¾ miles/2.8km
Height gain: 1020ft/310m
Time: 1 hour

The path starts to the left of the toilet block, and goes under the bridge of the old railway before climbing through Cwm Bychan with its little stream to the right. After a short climb the path continues past the iron pylons of the aerial cableway. Above, the pylons fork left off the main path on a grass path feeding through a grass, heather and bracken hollow.

Keep left as you come to a maze of off-shoot paths. Soon the route is confronted by a big craggy knoll ahead and a slightly lower ridge to the left. A grassy path climbs to a high pass between the two. Ignore paths on the right and those going over to the north-west edge. Instead follow the narrower ridge-top path, which climbs to the cairned summit of Mynydd Sygun.

Opposite: On Route MSN23, Cwm Bychan to Mynydd Sygun.

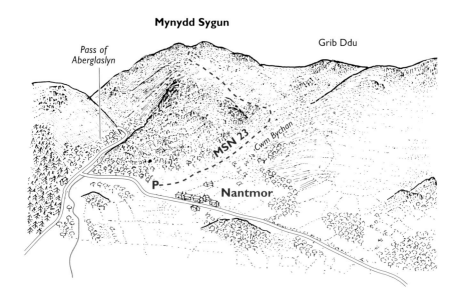

Route MSN24
Beddgelert

A steep and rugged route
Start: Beddgelert village car park
   (GR: SH 587481)
Distance: ¾ mile/1.3km
Height gain: 870ft/265m
Time: ½ hour

From the village car park return to the main road and turn left, past the shops and cafés to the near side of the pretty two-arched stone bridge over the Colwyn river. Don't cross but go straight ahead on the narrow lane past the Tanronnen Inn, the tea garden and craft shops, to cross the Afon Glaslyn on a tubular steel footbridge.

Again go straight on until you reach a fine terrace of cottages, where you turn right, then left along the lane at the far end. After a few paces, turn right by a footpath sign to pass Penlan cottage, the former home of Alfred Bestall, the illustrator of the *Rupert Bear* books. A rough rocky path beyond it tackles the steep slopes above the cottages and winds among rhododendrons.

After going through a metal kissing gate turn half-right on a steep stony path climbing through rhododendrons and heather right to the summit cairn on Mynydd Sygun's summit.

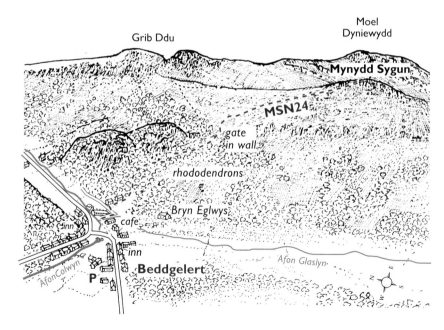

Other route options

A well-defined route from behind the Sygun
Copper Mines building rakes right up slopes
of rhododendron to join the ridge at the
ridge-crest cairn (GR 600479). From here a
narrow ridge-crest path leads south-west to
the summit.

RIDGE ROUTES

Moel Dyniewyd

Distance: 1⅓ miles/2.2km
Height gain: 525ft/160m
Time: ¾ hour

Follow the ridge crest down to a large cairn
(GR 600479), where a slightly wider path
continues along the Nantgwynant side of the
ridge. Take the right fork path climbing back
to the ridge beneath the great rocky knoll of
Crib Ddu, which towers above a deep grassy
hollow. A winding path climbs through
Bwlch y Sygun. Near the top of the pass
there's a large crag to negotiate, but there are
good footholds.

Over a ladder stile the path comes to a
junction. Turn right (south-east) to reach
another ladder stile. This time don't cross it
but take a narrower path that stays fairly close
to the fence. Beyond a shallow depression
and small lake, the path climbs up steep
craggy slopes to the summit of Moel
Dyniewyd.

Above: Beddgelert from Mynydd Sygun.

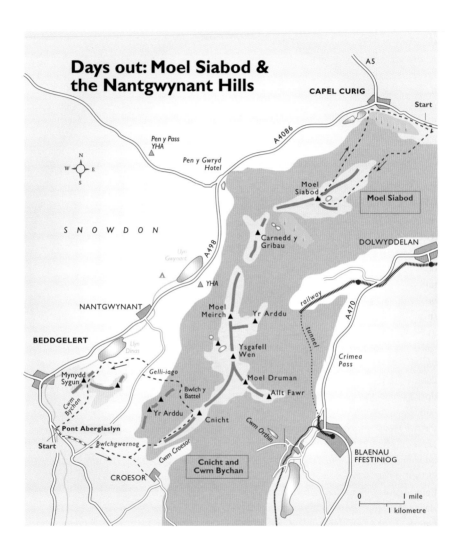

Days out: Moel Siabod & the Nantgwynant Hills

A5

CAPEL CURIG

Start

Pen y Pass
YHA

Pen y Gwryd
Hotel

A4086

Moel
Siabod

Moel Siabod

DOLWYDDELAN

N
W · E
S

S N O W D O N

Llyn
Gwynant

A498

YHA

Carnedd y
Gribau

railway

tunnel

NANTGWYNANT

Moel
Meirch

Yr Arddu

A470

Crimea
Pass

BEDDGELERT

Llyn
Dinas

Ysgafell
Wen

Mynydd
Sygun

Gelli-iago

Cwm
Bychan

Bwlch y
Battel

Moel Druman

Allt Fawr

Yr Arddu

Cnicht

Cwm Orthin

Pont Aberglaslyn

Start

Bwlchgwernog

Cwm Croesor

Cnicht and
Cwm Bychan

BLAENAU
FFESTINIOG

CROESOR

0   1 mile
1 kilometre

Days out: Moel Siabod & the Nantgwynant Hills

Moel Siabod

A single-minded circular route up
  Nantgwynant's highest mountain

Start: Car park behind the Pinnacle Café
  (GR: SH 720582)
Distance: 8 miles/13km
Height gain: 2850ft/870m
Time: 4½–5 hours

Take the track from the back of the car park leading away from Capel Curig, then turn left on the track at Gelli farm. This leads to the road opposite Llynnau Mymbyr. Turn left along the road towards the Plas y Brenin outdoor centre before, just short of the complex, turning right on a path leading over the footbridge spanning Nant Gwryd at the point the stream filters into Llynnau Mymbyr.

Beyond it turn left on a forest track that stays just inside the northern perimeters of the woodland of Coed Bryn-engan. The track comes to a footbridge over the Afon Llugwy – do not cross. Instead follow the riverside path, which traverses meadowland to reach the road at Pont Cyfyng where there are some waterfalls beneath a small stone-built road bridge.

Turn right to climb on the tarmac lane before taking the second footpath on the right, a private road passing more cottages before it degenerates into a rough stony quarry track. This climbs steadily uphill, with the cone of Moel Siabod rising from stark moorland. As the track ends a prominent path continues, tucking in left of a rocky spur thrown out by the mountain.

It traverses rough peaty slopes and passes a pleasant unnamed lake before coming across the derelict Rhos quarries. Beyond the old barracks the path passes left of a deep quarry pool and climbs more peaty slopes to look down on Llyn y Foel, a fine large tarn shaded by the immense rocky slopes of Siabod.

The path becomes intermittent as it struggles with the marshy ground to the north-west of the tarn, but soon reaches terra firma on Siabod's south-east spur. Be careful not to miss the turning up the rocky spur here, for the path you're on continues beyond the spur and loses itself on the mountain's southern slopes.

The spur is an exhilarating climb right to the summit – and what a view you get from the top rocks! The complete Snowdon Horseshoe can be seen across sylvan Nantgwynant, while Glyder Fach's bristly rocks and Tryfan's distinctive buttresses add a little spice to the view across Nant Gwryd, with the rolling Carneddau filling the rest of the horizon.

The way down starts unsurely. Ignore the rocky ridge top, but stay just to the left of it on the short grass. Eventually an increasingly bold path rakes NNE down the left side of the spur. The path becomes cairned and once over a ladder stile descends heather hillsides alongside the edge of a conifer forest with the white walls of the National Mountaineering

Centre of Plas y Brenin prominent in the valley below.

Eventually you enter the forest with a small stream to the left. On reaching a forestry track turn left, then leave it after a few paces for a path descending right and towards the Mymbyr Lakes. Go across the bridge over the outflow of the lake and climb to the road just left of Plas y Brenin.

Turn left for a short way before climbing the ladder stile on the right-hand side of the road. Take the higher of two tracks swinging right. This hugs the foot of the southern Glyder slopes. Beyond Gelli farm turn right to follow the cart track back to the car park.

Cnicht and Cwm Bychan

Follow a Roman road to the Matterhorn of Wales

Start: Pont Aberglaslyn car park
  (GR: SH 597462)
Distance: 11¼ miles/18km
Height gain: 3650ft/1110m
Time: 6 hours

Head back to the road from the car park and turn left (with care, it's quite busy at times). Leave the main road on the left for the lane passing through Nantmor and its pretty cottages. The undulating road then passes through woodland. Just beyond the crossing of the Nantmor stream at Bwlchgwernog the road comes to a junction with the Nantgwynant road. Staggered to the right you'll see a rough cart track raking up the slopes ahead. This is the course of Sarn Helen, a Roman road that ran the length of Wales.

The old road soon turns sharp left and traverses open country of crag and bracken. There are splendid retrospective views of Moel Hebog and the Nantlle Ridge, while the rugged Yr Arddu crags add a little spice to the view ahead. Soon a conical rock peak peers at you from over the horizon – it's the unmistakable shape of Cnicht. This 'Matterhorn of Wales' gets more impressive with each step.

At a junction of tracks (GR 628451) turn left. You're now on the popular Croesor route

Opposite: Descending the low slopes of Moel Siabod into the forests of Capel Curig, with the Carneddau peaks of Pen Llithrig y Wrach and Creigiau Gleision capturing the golden rays of twilight.

to Cnicht. A waymarker highlights a right turn off the track. Over the next stile the path climbs left (NE) with Cnicht in full view ahead. In the early stages the path keeps to the north (left) side of the ridge's crest, but eventually takes to the crest with spectacular views down crag and scree slopes into Cwm Croesor. On the far side of the cwm, Moelwyn Mawr, the highest peak in these parts, rises as a rounded dome from a long, low grassy ridge.

The route steepens and two narrow paths form (either will do) and clamber among the rocks of the summit massif. All too soon you're at the top looking along an undulating grass ridge whose sides are scraped with crag and scree. Little tarns are scattered on high plateaux while anonymous, little-known hills spread out across the horizon to reach their zenith at the gracefully sloped peak of Moel Siabod.

Set in a shallow grassy hollow below to the left and surrounded by low craggy outcrops, Llyn Biswail is particularly pleasing to the eye – somehow it always seems bluer than its neighbouring pools. The route will eventually descend past this on the journey back to base. First continue north-eastwards along the Cnicht ridge until the path reaches a cairn overlooking Llyn yr Adar, a large lake with an island in the centre – this is the 631m spot height on OS Explorer maps.

The next section is pathless. Leave the path at the cairn and contour left to a vague col beneath the rock knoll of Foel Boethwel. Now descend left to Llyn Biswail following

its south-east shores and then its outlet stream. This course descends through a craggy corridor towards the wild pass of Bwlch y Battel.

Ignore the nearer of two ladder stiles and keep a drystone wall to the right. Head south-west across rough grassland towards a ladder stile at the pass (GR 638472), where the route meets the prominent Bwlch y Battel–Gelli-iago path – using this second stile avoids the need for crossing the main stream where it is too wide and fast-flowing.

The route now descends on a clear path towards the Nantmor Valley. It stays to the south-west of the main stream and provides absolutely wonderful views of Snowdon and the Watkin Path as it eases down towards Gelli-iago. In the later stages the path gets steeper and winds down towards the cottage, now the Nantmor Adventure Centre. Go across the bridge over the stream and through a gate, keeping to the right of the cottage as you round it on to a drive that takes the route down to the Nantmor Road.

Turn right along the road for half a mile to the whitewashed house on the left, a converted chapel. A footpath to the left of it traverses rough pastureland then past the cottage of Hafod Owen. After entering the shade of woodland the path descends to Llyn Dinas, a beautiful lake whose shores of rush and rock are surrounded by craggy knolls, trimmed with woodland and bracken. The distinctive peaks of Yr Aran and Moel Hebog form the skyline across the lake towering above the wooded knoll of Dinas Emrys.

Turn left and follow the path along the southern shores of Dinas, rounding its western end beneath the craggy northern spur of Mynydd Sygun.

On reaching the lake's southern tip, leave the path for one that climbs the hillside to the left. The path winds up a heathery hollow to reach the old mine levels at Grib Ddu where the path divides. Take the path on the left to another ladder stile, which should be scaled before following a descending path through a craggy hollow, Cwm Bychan.

This passes the remains of copper mines and a row of rusting pylons, relics of an aerial cableway used to transport the ore to the Glaslyn valley. The path passes beneath a bridge carrying the Welsh Highland Railway and you may well be lucky enough to see one of their old steam trains chugging along the track that links Porthmadog and Caernarfon.

Beyond the bridge the path returns you to the car park at Pont Aberglaslyn.

Below: Hafod Owen, an isolated cottage on the slopes above Llyn Dinas.
Overleaf: Descending from Cnicht to Gelli-iago, with Snowdon ahead beyond Nantgwynant.

MAPS

Ordnance Survey Explorer (1:25 000)
  OL 17 Snowdonia: Snowdon
  OL 18 Snowdonia: Harlech,
  Porthmadog/Bala
Harveys Superwalker (1:25 000)
  Snowdonia: Snowdon & Moelwynion
  Snowdonia: the Glyderau & the
  Carneddau
BMC British Mountain Maps (1:40 000)
  Eryri/Snowdonia
Ordnance Survey Landranger (1:50 000)
  Sheet 115 Snowdon
  Sheet 124 Porthmadog & Dolgellau

TRANSPORT

Buses

Sherpa Buses, which are run by Gwynedd
  Council and Conwy County Borough
  Council with support from the Snowdonia
  National Park Authority, offer a
  comprehensive network through the
  mountain valleys. They allow the walker
  to select some excellent linear walks
  rather than contrived circulars to get back
  to a car. Buses run from Llandudno,
  Betws y Coed, Bangor, Bethesda,
  Caernarfon, Llanberis and Porthmadog
  into the heart of the Snowdonian
  mountains.
Bus timetable:
  www.gwynedd.gov.uk/bwsgwynedd

Trains

Llandudno, Llandudno Junction, Conwy,
  Penmaenmawr, Llanfairfechan and Bangor
  are all served by the North Wales Coast
  Line, while the Blaenau Ffestiniog branch
  line from Llandudno Junction has stations
  throughout the Conwy and Lledr Valleys,
  including Llanrwst, Betws y Coed,
  Dolwyddelan and Roman Bridge.
Rail travel timetable (Railtrack):
  www.nationalrail.co.uk
For more information: www.traveline-
  cymru.org.uk

ACCOMMODATION AND SUPPLIES

Tourist Information Centres (year round)

Beddgelert
  Tel. 01766 890615
  Email: tic.beddgelert@eryri-npa.gov.uk
Betws y Coed
  Tel. 01690 710426
  Email: tic.byc@eryri-npa.gov.uk
Blaenau Ffestiniog
  Tel. 01766 830360
  Email: tic.blaenau@eryri-npa.gov.uk
Conwy
  Tel. 01492 592248
  Email: conwy@nwtic.com

Websites

Welsh Tourist Board: www.visitwales.com
Snowdonia information:
  www.visitsnowdonia.info
Accommodation: www.4tourism.com

BEST BASES

Bangor This pleasant university city on the shores of the Menai Straits has good accommodation and speedy road links to Aber and Llanfairfechan, the resorts best placed for routes into the northern Carneddau. There are plenty of shops and supermarkets.

Beddgelert Beautifully sited by the confluence of the Colwyn and the Glaslyn and beneath the more verdant and sylvan slopes of Snowdon, Beddgelert, with its twin-arched bridge and pretty stone cottages, makes an ideal base for the Nantgwynant Hills, including Moel Meirch and Ysgafell Wen. There are a couple of camp sites and very high-standard country house hotels and several B&Bs. Walkers can tackle Moel Dyniewyd and Mynydd Sygun from the village.

Bethesda Although it doesn't seem to attempt to cater for tourists, Bethesda has good shops for restocking. The nearby Snowdon Lodge has plenty of accommodation and welcomes walkers. Bethesda is ideally placed for the western and southern Carneddau approaches. On the Carneddau slopes above Bethesda lies the village of **Gerlan,** where an old school has been converted to a private hostel, Caban Cysgu. This is very handy for both the Cwm Caseg and Cwm Llafar routes.

Betws y Coed Pronounced something like 'bettuz ee koyd', this large and bustling village is set by an equally bustling river, the Llugwy, not far from its confluence with the Afon Conwy. Betws has scores of B&Bs and many hotels. It's a good place for renewing supplies, with a choice of grocers, bakers and several gear shops. It is reasonably handy for the eastern Carneddau and the narrow roads into the hills around Llyn Crafnant and Figiau.

Capel Curig This linear village straddles the A5 in small huddles of cottages for about three miles. It has a few good hotels and B&Bs, a youth hostel and a camp site. There are a couple of outdoor gear shops too. The Pinnacle Café at the junction of the A5 and the A4088 is a meeting place for many walkers and climbers before and after their forays into the mountains. It is well placed for routes on the southern Carneddau, and all of the Glyderau.

Conwy Sited between the Carneddau's northern reaches and the sea, with town walls, a castle by the fishing harbour and a modern marina, Conwy offers walkers a chance to relax in fascinating surroundings when they've had a day on the hills. Walkers can step out of their B&Bs straight on to Conwy Mountain. The town offers a wide variety of accommodation, including hotels, B&Bs and caravan sites (no camp sites any more – the nearest is at Dwygyfylchi).

Dolwyddelan In the heart of the Lledr Valley, scenic Dolwyddelan is famous for its hilltop castle. It has a couple of inns and B&Bs and a camp site, is accessible by railway and bus, and is an ideal base for eastern approaches to Moel Siabod and the Nantgwynant Hills.

Llanberis Snowdonia's biggest mountain village has hotels from large to small, B&Bs, cafés and varied shops. Pete's Eats has been described as 'the best chippy in the world'. The large and lively village is handily placed for the Llanberis Pass routes up the Glyderau. **Nant Peris**, its smaller neighbour, has two camp sites catering mainly for tents. The Vaynol Arms is a very good pub.

Llanfairfechan The Victorian resort of Llanfairfechan hasn't as much accommodation as it had in the past, but there are a few B&Bs scattered around, along with a couple of cafés on the promenade and a handful of shops.

Llanrwst This attractive riverside market town has a couple of hotels, a camp site and a few B&Bs. There are takeaways and cafés as well as a good variety of shops. Llanrwst along with nearby **Trefriw** is a good place for explorations of the eastern Carneddau, including Cwm Eigiau and Tal y Fan.

Nantgwynant This tiny hamlet of a few cottages, a youth hostel (Bryngwynant) and camp site is set among the stunning scenery of the Glaslyn Valley between the lakes of Dinas and Gwynant. It's a good base for explorations of Moel Meirch, Ysgafell Wen, Craig Llyn-llagi and Cnicht and only a short bus ride away from start points for Moel Siabod.

Penmaenmawr/Dwygyfylchi A Victorian seaside resort, Penmaenmawr's town has become a bit down-at-heel, not helped by the modern A55 which has tourists speeding by without a second glance. Things have improved recently, and the town is very handily placed for an exploration of Tal y Fan and its ancient circles and burial mounds. **Dwygyfylchi** is set in a pleasant pastoral hollow between the coast and the Sychnant Pass, ideal for Tal y Fan and Conwy Mountain. Together, the two resorts have a camp site, a caravan site, B&Bs, inns and a few shops.

Rowen Little Rowen, which lies in a pastoral hollow between the foothills of the Carneddau and the Conwy Valley, is chocolate-box pretty, with whitewashed cottages, tea houses and rose gardens. It has an excellent pub, a couple of very fine country house hotels and a youth hostel, which is a mile or so uphill towards Tal y Fan. The village is a lovely out-of-the-way find, and is great for explorations deep into the northern Carneddau.

YOUTH HOSTELS

Bangor
Tan-y-Bryn, Bangor LL57 1PZ
Tel. 0870 770 5686
Email: bangor@yha.org.uk

Betws y Coed
Swallow Falls, Betws y Coed LL24 0DW
Tel. 01690 710796
Email: betwsycoed@yha.org.uk

Capel Curig
Plas Curig, Capel Curig,
Betws-y-Coed LL24 0EL
Tel. 0870 770 5746
Email: capelcurig@yha.org.uk

Conwy
Larkhill, Sychnant Pass Road,
Conwy LL32 8AJ
Tel. 0870 770 6111
Email: conwy@yha.org.uk

Llanberis
Llwyn Celyn, Llanberis LL55 4SR
Tel. 0870 770 5928
Email: llanberis@yha.org.uk

Nantgwynant
Bryngwynant, Nantgwynant,
Caernarfon LL55 4NP
Tel. 0870 770 5732
Email: bryngwynant@yha.org.uk

FURTHER INFORMATION

Nant Ffrancon/Ogwen
Idwal Cottage, Nant Ffrancon, Bethesda,
  Bangor LL57 3LZ
Tel. 0870 770 5874
Email: idwal@yha.org.uk

Pen-y-Pass
Nantgwynant, Caernarfon LL55 4NY
Tel. 0870 770 5990
Email: penypass@yha.org.uk

Rowen
Rhiw Farm, Rowen, near Conwy LL32 8YW
Tel. 01492 650089

YHA National Office
Trevelyan House, Dimple Road, Matlock,
  Derbyshire DE4 3YH
Tel. 0870 770 8868
Website: www.yha.org.uk

THE WELSH LANGUAGE

Some Welsh words

aber	river mouth
afon	river
arddu	black crag
bach/fach	small
bedd	grave
betws	chapel
blaen	head of valley
bont/pont	bridge
bwlch	pass
bws	bus
cae	field
caer	fort
carn/carnedd/garn/garnedd	cairn/cairns
capel	chapel
carreg/garreg	stone
castell	castle
cefn	ridge
cors/gors	bog
clogwyn	cliff
coch/goch	red
coeden/coed	tree/wood
craig/graig	crag
crib	sharp ridge
cwm	coomb
cwn	dog
Cymru/Cymraeg	Wales/Welsh
dinas	hill fort (or town)
diolch	thank you
du/ddu	black
drum/trum	ridge
drws	door
dyffryn	valley
dwr	water

eglwys	church
esgair	ridge
eryri	eagles' abode
fawr/mawr	large
felin/melin	mill
ffordd	road
ffynnon	spring
ffridd	enclosed grazing land
glas/las	blue
gwrydd	green
gwyn	white
gwynt	wind
hafod	high-altitude summer dwelling
hendre	winter dwelling
isaf	lower
llan	church or blessed place
llwybr cyhoeddus	public footpath
llwyd	grey
llyn	lake
maen	stone
maes	field/meadow
melyn	yellow
moch	pig
moel/foel	featureless hill
mynydd	mountain
nant	stream
ogof	cave
pant	clearing, hollow
pen	peak
person	cascade
plas	mansion
pwll	pool
rhaeadr	waterfall
rhyd	ford
saeth(au)	arrow(s)
troed	foot of
twll	hole, fracture, broken
ty	house
uchaf	high, higher
waun	moor
wen	white
wrach	witch
y, yr	the
ynys	island

Pronunciation of consonants

c   always hard, like the English 'k', thus coed = 'koyd'
ch   as in the Scottish 'loch'
dd   a voiced 'th' as in 'booth'
f   like the English 'v' , thus fach = 'vach'
ff   like the English 'f'
ll   a Scots 'ch' followed by an 'l' (blow air out between your tongue and your top teeth when pronouncing)

Pronunciation of vowels

w   can be a consonant or a vowel. When working as a vowel, pronounced like 'oo' as in 'cook' or 'moon'.
y   can be a consonant or a vowel. When working as a vowel, pronounced like 'i' as in pin or 'ee' as in seen. U is exactly the same.

The letters j, k, q, v, x and z are not used in true Welsh words.